John Colquhoun

Sporting days

John Colquhoun

Sporting days

ISBN/EAN: 9783742898654

Manufactured in Europe, USA, Canada, Australia, Japa

Cover: Foto ©Suzi / pixelio.de

Manufactured and distributed by brebook publishing software
(www.brebook.com)

John Colquhoun

Sporting days

SPORTING DAYS

BY

JOHN COLQUHOUN

AUTHOR OF

'THE MOOR AND THE LOCH,' 'SALMON-CASTS AND
STRAY SHOTS,' ETC.

WILLIAM BLACKWOOD AND SONS
EDINBURGH AND LONDON
MDCCCLXVI

PREFACE.

—

EXCEPTING the Northern tour, the following articles were contributed to an Edinburgh weekly journal anxious to establish a sporting sheet. The introduction will explain its object. The whole comprises a few of the last experiences of the Author's shooting and fishing life.

In these later days he has consequently had the pleasure and comfort of always being accompanied by one or other, sometimes by both his two elder sons, who, having been thoroughly trained by himself, never annoyed him by mistakes or blunders, which so often ruffle the old hand when in company with a young brother of the rod or gun.

One of these dear companions is now shooting bears, antelopes, wild peacocks, &c., in India, with his regiment, "the old Black Watch;" while his elder brother has also found a congenial field in "the sister island," where for the last five years he has been serving with the Royal Irish Dragoon Guards.

A first Indian addition to the home museum was an eagle flying over the tents when the young hunter opportunely had his fowling-piece in hand. He shortly after added another trophy in the portly person of a brown bear, killed by a little double Whitworth given him on departure.

On the first shooting-party Bruin was stealing along a ledge of rocks, at the base of which the rifle was posted. The bear rolled down the precipice and pitched at the shooter's feet. Fortunately the shot was deadly, or the rough one might have acknowledged the salute by a too cordial embrace. These and numerous other foreign spoils are preserved to adorn the joint collection.

The Author has only further to say that all his sporting feats are transcripts from his private journal, taken down the same night, or at furthest next morning after they occurred. He has never, therefore, been forced to draw on memory—or imagination!

KAMES CASTLE, *July* 1866.

CONTENTS.

	PAGE
INTRODUCTION,	1
SEA-FOWL SHOOTING IN THE FIRTH OF FORTH,	7
DEER-DRIVING IN MULL,	33
LOCH SALMON-FISHING,	67
SEAL-SHOOTING,	81
NATURAL HISTORY AND SPORT OF BUTE,	96
GLENFALLOCH ROES,	160
AUTUMN ANGLING ON THE LYON,	185
A PTARMIGAN DAY,	211
THE COMMON DOTTEREL,	232
THE WILDS OF SUTHERLAND: ALTNAHARRA—DURNESS —SCOURIE—INCHNADAMFF,	239

SPORTING RECOLLECTIONS.

INTRODUCTION.

THE superiority in pluck and endurance of hardship which the British Islands have so long held over the other nations of Europe is pretty generally admitted to be in no small degree due to the love and practice of our out-of-door recreations. Nowhere is this more fully acknowledged than in our army, where year by year additional facilities are given to colonels of regiments from headquarters to permit those under them as much sporting leave as is consistent with attention to duty. Many of our most distinguished commanders have openly expressed their opinion, that although a man who devotes all his time and

A

energy to military duty may be an excellent and valuable parade officer, yet in actual service, when anything dashing was done, it was, in nine cases out of ten, by those who loved the hunting-field or the grouse-mountain far better than the barrack-square, and that these were generally the most efficient officers in an arduous campaign.

The impetus given to the mental as well as the physical powers by healthy exercise no one denies, though hundreds profess themselves unable (more truly, perhaps, unwilling) to submit to the arduous experiment. An ordinary walk is not enough for a strong man who is at the same time an earnest student. In order to keep his mind up to the mark, he ought to accustom himself to hardship, and inure his limbs and muscles to fatigue. No doubt it is *hard laws* to a man in middle life, who has never done more than his "Saturday's walk," and a short stroll the other days of the week, to send him up the steep mountain-side with a gun under his arm; but even he, by perseverance and practice, will be astonished at his own powers, and delighted with the probable result—health and strength of mind and body.

It is needless to say how few of us would endure this continual hardship and fatigue, were it not for the present excitement, which impetus is supplied by the love of hunting, innate, though often latent, in most manly and independent characters. I always sympathised with the Scotch poacher of fifty years ago, who, for the sheer love of sport, sallied out over the well-known hills, and with his quaintly broke collie dog and rusty single-barrel enjoyed himself to the full. *He* never sold his game, but when he had more than his family could use, gave the rest to his neighbours. That is past and gone ; the English squire first drove the poorer Scotch one out of the market, and he in his turn has been superseded by the millionaires from London, Manchester, and America. Incredible prices are given by the latter for all our first-class deer forests and shootings, while the second-rate beats are as eagerly contended for by the men of less ample means ; and now it is Sassenachs, protection, and keepers over the whole Highland range. This picture may not be a very bright one to a high-spirited and patriotic Scotchman : still it has its light as well as shade. The almost fabulous rents paid for all the best beats brings money into the country, and the sportsmen, to say nothing of being fleeced by the natives, are lavish of their purses, which also swells the stream of wealth flowing into the Highlands. To recur to my opening sentence, not a few fine aristocratic young Englishmen, who without this rugged attraction would have been confined to the hunting-field, stubbles, and turnips, are initiated into the more hardening and fatiguing sports of the deer-forests and the grouse-moors. These are the young fellows to endure privations and suffer hardship: they have done it before for amusement, and can do it again for duty.

Highland touring was in vogue long before the *furore* for its wild sports began, and to the "Lord of the buried past" we owe the interest first excited in the northern wilds. A Scotch tour, however, was in those days an expensive and often very uncomfortable luxury. Most of our southern neighbours were quite content with one trial, feeling satisfied they had seen enough of the uncultivated region and its savages to last them all their lives. But when the country was thrown open by steamboats and railways, and the natural consequences of better inns and conveyances—above all, when good shootings at very moderate prices were in the market, no wonder that even the cream of England's aristocracy looked forward to their autumn sojourn in the North as the most charming portion of the whole year.

Thirty years ago there were no Scotch sporting books, and the few English ones were merely works of instruction and dry detail. Now, however, the Scotch books on mountain, forest, and river sport occupy no mean place in our national literature. How much these books stimulated the demand for Scotch shootings it would be difficult to say; at all events, wild shooting rose prodigiously in the market after their publication. Thirty years since capital small ranges were to be had for £150 to £180. The rapidity with which these rose to thrice that amount was most disheartening to keen grouse-shooters of moderate incomes. The competition for the first-class beats was even greater, and I have been told by agents that the claimants bid each other up to such a figure that they were sometimes ashamed to take the highest offer.

Not many years ago there was always a tempting array of shooting quarters advertised in February and March. At present, all the most desirable quarters are secured before coming into the market at all. The man of fortune who comes down to the North in early spring, reasonably confident of finding a really good shooting, has often to return sadly disappointed: there are none to be had for *love* or *money*.

Since, then, Highland sport has done so much for Scotland, and created such great interest even in England, it seems curious that no sporting paper has yet been established in the capital of the North. The journal, therefore, alluded to in the preface, arranged to reserve a weekly sheet, and take in *seriatim* the whole *rôle* of field, forest, moor, river, loch, and ocean, feeling confident that the contributions would never fail for lack of material attractive, exciting, and romantic.

SEA-FOWL SHOOTING IN THE FIRTH OF FORTH.

WE have long discovered two distinct and widely different classes amongst men who are fond of recreation with the gun. By far the most numerous type are mere shooting-machines, whose delight is a partridge or grouse *drive,* when the honours of the day are accorded to him who has the largest heap of dead birds at his feet. The plan of the campaign is simple enough. A row of guns take up a position under the mask of a wall, hedge, or drain, crossing the line where the driven birds are sure to fly. A large number of beaters are sent round to raise the game, which keep constantly dashing past, or over the heads of the sportsmen. When all the partridge or grouse are moved in one direction, the shooters wheel to the right about, and the flight is again driven from the opposite quarter. No doubt this requires good and very quick shooting, but so does the *battue* and the pigeon-trap; and for our own part, we see little difference in these three lazy and luxurious modes of bird butchery.

The other class to whom we allude, so far as our own experience goes, are far less numerous. They have little sympathy with these massacres; and, although regarding quick and true shooting as the first requisite, it is no more than the *first*— the A B C of sporting with the gun.

To feel the superiority of a man of this stamp, you require to see him out over a rugged country, where game is not over plentiful, and when the November blasts have made it wild and wary. The complete self-reliance, caution, and care with which he will give his beautifully trained dogs the benefit of all the best spots to harbour game; the knowing manner he will approach it when found; the masterly way he will spring the pack or covey to advantage; and the exquisitely quick and steady shooting—so essential when game

is strong and shy—make an empty bag to a
shooter with the above qualifications a rare event.
It is evident, however, that none can possess them
without long experience and acute observation,
advantages which have most likely enticed the
possessor into the tempting province of the naturalist. A new field has thus been opened up. The
sportsman studies the nature and habits of the
wild creatures of chase, not merely to get shots at
them, but also for the pleasure derived from the
study itself. In place of being confined to the
shooting months, *his* sporting season comprises
the whole year. The advent and departure of
migrants ; the discovery of a rare visitor, with
perhaps the triumph of adding him to the museum ;
the inexpressible delight and excitement of a trip
to the crags and cliffs of the ocean, swarming with
their varieties of wild sea-birds, with wilder cries,
are now objects of even greater interest than his
most successful day among the grouse or the deer.

The time for studying the peculiar and individual characteristics of sea-fowl is the month of
May. Not only are the birds tamer then, and
their instincts more prominently brought out, but

each species is decked in its most imposing and brightest attire. From a lightly-rigged yawl on a sunny May morning with a gentle breeze, the *coup d'œil* of a coast, well frequented by sea-birds, and in the neighbourhood of their breeding-rocks, is the most absorbing of all marine views. You see the countless array of guillemots, razor-bills, sea-parrots, cormorants, and grebes—some diving at your approach, others rising in your wake, numbers darting on wing, a fair though quick cross-shot, past the bow or stern of your trig little craft ; an infinite variety of gulls, from the giant to the kittywake, flapping lazily over and around you, and the solan in the distance, just poising, then coming down prone like a meteor into the glancing wave, the dull thud of the plunge being heard at a mile's distance. Soaring among them from her secure nest among the most fearful of the beetling cliffs is the sooty raven, scarcely, however, to be distinguished, but by her croak, from a jackdaw ; while the peregrine, also nidifying on a giddy point, and faring sump-tuously on her sea neighbours, seems dwarfed to a merlin.

Amidst this magnificent but, to the uninitiated, chaotic panorama, we have placed the occupant of the picturesque fishing-boat, and will suppose him a keen sportsman just lapsing into the naturalist. Anxious for rare specimens, but totally bewildered, he turns helplessly to the boatmen, who overpower him, as the fowl dash past, with the coast slang nicknames — Marrots, Tommie Nories, Nettle-ducks, Coll-the-caunle-wicks, Letter-o'-marques, &c.—until, perhaps, the day closes with a boat-load of trash, and only some distant random chances at the wilder, rarer, or more gorgeous treasures of the deep.

How vastly intensified in interest does this living sea become to the keen eye of an experienced sportsman, who is at the same time an accomplished naturalist. Not only does he know each kind and genus by book, but from an intimate knowledge of their habits and manners, and a quick eye kept in constant practice, can distinguish every variety at distances which (to a novice) appear impossible. He scans the sea with his telescope, detects at a glance the specimens he is in search of, and immediately decides upon the safest approach that

offers a fair prospect of a successful shot. Should
he secure the coveted object of pursuit, it is not
alone its rarity or beauty which makes his heart
to dance like his little shallop over the waves, but
the associations sure to cling to it in future and
far distant years. To him each of those sea-birds
that grace his museum suggests its own wild tale
of grandeur or beauty. The beetling precipice,
the gleaming, tranquil sea, the jutting headland,
or booming, boundless old ocean, rise to his mind's
eye, fresh and glorious, even by a passing glance
at that little denizen of the deep.

The North Berwick fisherman had written to
say that eiders were plentiful, and had begun to
seek the nesting islands in the Firth. Accompanied by my eldest son, and armed with our
shoulder duck-guns, we were next morning early
afloat for a cruise in search of them. The day
was bright, but the breeze perhaps rather too
fresh to give us full advantage in manœuvring
wild fowl. We soon sighted several flocks of
snowy drakes with their russet partners; but from
bearing too eagerly down upon them, raised them
all out of reach of even a cross-shot. Like all

other game, wild-fowl have their fidgety moods,
sometimes without any apparent cause. This
morning, the eiders being shy and "fretty" on
water, we ran down to the islet of Fiddery, hoping
for a stalking-shot from the land. Although we
expected any feeding or resting fowl would be
moored in the sheltered bays, we first made sure
of the exposed shore with our glasses, and then
noiselessly and stealthily landed on it. Directly
opposite was a tiny bay—a favourite haunt, with
the wind in the quarter in which it then was.
The approach was simple, and, to an experienced
shot, certain. When I got to the top of the rock
immediately above, as I expected, there were
about a dozen ducks and drakes diving and sporting in joyous security. A sheer descent of seventy
yards rather cooled my eagerness to fire, well
knowing that even with my trusty "Ross" gun
this was a most uncertain shot. Choosing a fine
drake, I fired, and he lay motionless on the water ;
but my second shot was not so fortunate, as the
bird aimed at flew rapidly round the island with
the rest.

The boatman soon fished up the dead bird, and

we beat up against the wind, looking out for a fresh chance. I was not long in espying a solitary white speck in the direct line of the team I had shot at, which I at once suspected was my second-barrel bird. Getting well to windward, we carefully bore down, and the eider, although uneasy, allowed us to run within reach of a long shot, then heavily rose, and hanging against the wind, crossed our bow. We fired together. The bird dropped, and instantly dived, but soon rose again to the surface—dead.

We had now secured two splendid eider drakes, but to complete the case a brown mate was needed for each. Again I scanned the wide expanse of water with the telescope, and soon fixed it on a large bird in the smooth water near the mainland coast. " It's the loon, sir," shouts the boatman ; "there's one of them has haunted these bays for the last fortnight." As I had no specimen yet, the Great Northern was a prize worth trying for. From their weakness in the air, and their amazing power in the water, grebes and divers are very unwilling to take wing, always preferring to baffle their foes in the element to which nature has so finely adapted them. The difficulty, therefore, of getting a shot consists in their jealousy of a close approach, and the power they all possess, by swimming very low, of slipping under water like magic.

The Great Northern is not only the most wary of the diving tribe, but his progress under water is as fast as that of some birds in the air, and the length of his dive often extends to a quarter of a mile. We therefore went to work very cautiously, first tacking about to windward for some time, to accustom the bird to the appearance of the boat, and then gently wearing her, we approached imperceptibly nearer and nearer. The loon was greedily feeding, and from the shortness of his dives, and the rapidity with which they succeeded each other, he had evidently an abundant feast. Crouching in the bow, with my gun at my shoulder, I was several times within long range; but either this quick-eyed grebe dipped down just as my finger touched the trigger, or his position was unfavourable for shot to penetrate the oily feathers. At last, however, I did get a fair chance at sixty yards, and the No. 3 dropped round him in perfect pattern. He was down in a twinkling, and did not show again for some time. We followed, but in vain, for each dive became longer the further we pursued—and little did I think that this king of divers had his death-wound, and would yet be mine. Two days after, some poor fishermen found him dead, and, when he was skinned, it was discovered that a No. 3 pellet had passed through one side of the head, and lodged above the eye on the other.

The chase after the Great Northern Diver had taken us out to sea again, and brought us nearly opposite the second islet of the group named " The Lamb." The eastern rocks are a favourite stance of the great cormorant, or " Scart," called by fishermen at the breeding season, " Letter-o'-marques," from the white patches on the top of each thigh. On the pinnacle of one of these rocks, which rise abruptly out of the water, like the Needles in the Isle of Wight, three were seated in state, sunning themselves luxuriously after their morning feed. There was little hope of a shot from the sea, but no difficulty in getting within seventy yards from the land. On gaining the rocks I had an interesting inspection of the trio, who were extending their long wings and preening their feathers in full enjoyment of the noonday sun.

Selecting the brightest coloured of the group, I fired from a rest, and the bird dropped into the waves, struggled for an instant on the top, then recovered and plunged down, his companions meanwhile flying out to sea. The boat being at the other side of the island, was some time in coming round, and either from the roughness of the sea, or from the cormorant having found a hiding-place on the shore, we never saw it again.

During the remainder of the day we tried every device, both on land and water, to procure at least one female eider, but failed, neither of two very distant chances from the boat being successful.

Next morning, the breeze having died away into a dead calm, we were reduced to " wooden sails," a mode of progress and approach relished neither by boatmen nor sea-fowl. At every curl on the distant blue the former waved and whistled for a breeze, but all in vain. They were forced to bend their unwilling backs to a three-mile pull for another search of Fiddery, with the poor prospect of a random shot by the way.

The sight and sound of a row-boat always put
wild-fowl on their guard, and generally stimulate
them to be alert and uneasy; so, notwithstanding
the frequent groups of eiders and scoters floating
all round on the quiet sea, the dip of the oars
scared each team far out of reach. Unfortunately,
also, the large flock of male and female eiders had
posted themselves *outside* the bays of Fiddery,
beyond the reach of shot. As they were most unlikely to move when the water was so smooth, we
had to change our tactics by taking post for a flying
chance, while the boatmen pulled round to drive
them, if possible, within range of our hiding-places.

A bluff of detached and jagged rock rising
abruptly in the sea, a little to the west of the
island, afforded me safe ambush, while my son
succeeded equally well in securing himself among
the rough stones of the Fiddery coast. We had
thus a narrow sea between us, where the fowl, if
judiciously flushed, would be very likely to pass
within reach of either gun, when rounding the west
corner of the island from its northern end, where
they were now seated.

A few detached birds dashing past in mid-channel, and of course out of reach, showed that the fishermen had succeeded in their task. The main body soon followed this advanced-guard. They simultaneously took wing, but soon separated into three groups. Two of these kept the island side, but the third flew straight for my rock. With eager heart and ready weapon I waited until they skimmed overhead, a quick but fair chance. A female eider dropped on the water to my shot, but seeing she was only winged, I was taking aim with my second barrel when she dived, and did not rise again within range.

Bang! bang! from the islet. My telescope was instantly fixed on my son. He was wading into the sea, where I distinctly saw him pick up a dead bird. Our boatmen, who had been straining hard, now pulled up to my stance, and at the same time my son was making signs to me in a certain direction, so, instead of pursuing my winged duck, we obeyed his signal, and soon spied a solitary bird, which proved a female eider. Upon nearing her she dived, but being hard hit in the body, soon came to the surface again, when we made her safe by a shot.

This happy right and left having supplied a companion to each of the eider drakes, we triumphed in anticipation of our collection being adorned with these superb examples of natural history. Could I have foreseen that ere the day closed another of these much-admired eiders would have deprived me of a shot at the rarest sea-bird I ever detected in the Firth, I might not have regarded them so complacently.

Having landed to search one of the homeward islands, a male eider was asleep on a promontory which flanked a tiny bay. A ledge of rocks, parallel to both, made the stalk after fowl either in this creek or on the promontory very easy. Neglecting (contrary to my wont) to examine the bay, I gave my whole notice to the unsuspecting drake, struck him badly at the sitting shot, and brought him down dead with the other.

Before I could rise from my hiding, three little sea-fowl swam rapidly into view from the bay. They never saw me, and seeming more surprised than frightened, never attempted to fly. The leader had a hood like a hoopoe, and in the centre of the hood a white star, the Hooded Merganser !

It was a tempting and mortifying moment to watch the little trio, within such fair distance at first, quickly paddle out of reach long before I was "shotted."

Leaving the eider where he fell, we were soon in full chase; but the American strangers had, on second thoughts, betaken themselves to their wings, when I ran to warn the men to bring the boat, and I have never fallen in with this rare mergus before or since. When we returned to pick up the dead drake, the fishermen, far from sympathising with my chagrin at losing such a prize, were firmly convinced that the eider ought to be ample consolation, and was by far the most valuable "fule" of the two.

With the exception of the black guillemot, and the great cormorant when dignified by his credentials, my museum now contained all the native sea-birds of the Firth of Forth. A pair or two of these sable guillemots sometimes hatch on the Island of May, whose dizzy crags also afford a secure night-roost to the scart, while its boisterous sea-coves are the favourite retreat of the green cormorant or shag. The distance of "the May" from North Berwick is eight miles, but it is necessary to be cautious in crossing this channel in an open boat, as a little wind soon raises a heavy sea.

My usual skipper, Glass, being absent at the herring-fishing, we hired the most sea-worthy fishing-smack in the harbour, belonging to his late pupil and assistant Kelly. Although there were some ugly streamers, what seamen call a "dirty" or "dusty" sky, yet the west wind was gentle, and perfectly fair for our destination, the lighthouse of May.

Kelly's crew was made up of his father-in-law, an old whale-fisher, and a stout lad who seemed to have been nourished on tobacco and whisky. When the sail was hoisted outside the docks, with the soft west wind just strong enough to fill it, and the Bass and Tantallon spread before us, with all their romantic associations, one's spirit rose as in earlier days. Even our crew appeared to share the enthusiasm—not the less, perhaps, from the good supply of meat, drink, and tobacco. If I *did* catch Kelly casting a furtive glance now and then at the streaky horizon, he seemed ashamed of himself; as for the old whaler, he regarded sea, sky, wind, everything with utter contempt, except the provision basket.

In sailing over to the May, the boat might have been freighted with the commoner kind of sea-birds, but we only shot a few for the boatmen. A pair of solans crossed the bow, when my son dropped both—a right and left shot—and they were cleverly netted as the boat sailed past. A third flew by the stern, which I killed, but being unwilling to lose time by tacking, we left it on the waves. We declined to shoot again at these geese, which may almost be termed private property.

The breeze had freshened, and the waves were high enough to make shooting difficult, and landsmen squeamish. The boat was, however, abreast of the south-west corner of the May, and we were about to hug the land in a search of the western rocks for cormorants and the black guillemot. The west wind, so friendly in the morning, was now a bitter foe, for it drove the surf upon the rocks in great booming billows, making it no easy task to discern the difference of sea-birds at any distance, and next to impossible to force the cormorants from the shelter of the caves. In a cavern less exposed to the rolling swell, a pair of shags were perched on a point of rock. The boatmen clapped their hands and shouted, but both birds dropped into the terrific boiling caldron below. They remained so long in this whirlpool that we fancied they had escaped out to sea. At last they emerged and took post on the same ledge. Kelly then threw a piece of wood at them. One dived, but the other flew out, and was shot by my son. As its neighbour did not show again in the cave, it no doubt escaped into the sea by a long underwater swim. The cormorant we secured was a male, in the richest green, with a spring tuft in perfection.

The black guillemot was not visible to-day, but a pair of peregrines flew out screaming from their eyrie, the sharp flicker of their wings contrasting with the solemn flap, flap of the seabirds.

The ebbing tide made our landing on the May for a trial of the cormorant roosts rather difficult. On our way we called at the lighthouse, and the keeper and his wife most civilly agreed to give us tea on our return from the rocks, and allowed us to eke it out by shooting a rabbit. A row of "Letter-o'-marques" were already drawn up on their night quarters. One of the nearest, decked in the most bright and varied colours, looked like their chief. Of course *he* was the target, but being fixed at far too long a range, dropped down the abyss with the rest, little inconvenienced by the No. 2. Had we not been so eager another overlooked approach would have abridged the distance by thirty yards, when most likely this brilliant specimen would have been ours. The only resource now was to take post above the rocks, and await the return of our fugitives. As dusk was setting in, they soon began to cross backwards and forwards at long distance. Fearing that darkness would stop our shooting, we were forced to try these random chances, which were all shotproof !

Seated at our snug meal in the lighthouse, Kelly appeared with rueful face. " The nicht," he said, " looked ugly, rain had set in, and they had much difficulty, from the surf and low tide, in getting our carpet-bags out of the boat." I suggested pulling her up on the beach, but Kelly shook his head. They could neither take her out of the water, nor come on shore themselves all night, lest she might be dashed in pieces. We therefore made the poor fellows as comfortable as we could by a bottle of whisky, some good table-beer, and an ample supply of food.

We begged our kind host to allow us to see the tower lighted. This was strictly against rules, but he at once agreed to let my son see the lights put out. As this ceremony took place at four in the morning, I was too sleepy to join it; but my son affirmed that a more startling and brilliant illumination he had never beheld.

A loud rap at six next morning, and Kelly's voice imploring us to leave our beds, roused me from a sound sleep. When the tide was full they had run the fishing-boat into a sheltered creek, but as it was ebbing fast we must embark in less than an hour, failing which the boat must be moved out to sea, and neither we nor our baggage might be able to get on board. Kelly added carelessly, but slyly, "There is a queer bird diving outside the creek where the boat is, that nane o' us kens what it is." This was a master-stroke. We were down in half the time stipulated, and immediately assured that the unknown was still at his post. I was completely puzzled. At first I fancied the bird a smew, but was corrected by the telescope. Cautiously shoving nearer and nearer with the boat-hook, the little diver at length began to sheer off. Now was the time to fire, and it lay dead to my son's shot—a black guillemot, but in the light speckled plumage of winter.

The sails were scarcely hoisted, when, in the distance, but flying towards us, I distinctly saw another of these guillemots, but this one was black as ebony. He crossed between us and the shore, about 300 yards from the boat. Both telescopes were fixed if possible to mark him down. He soon plumped into the water, and every time the wave rose we had a full view of the black speck on its crest. The jumble of the sea made shooting uncertain, but I still pre-

ferred a long chance to the probability of flush-
ing the bird out of reach by coming sharply down
for a closer one.   Kelly, as usual, steered to perfection, and brought our craft down abreast of
the prize in the exact line I had pointed out.
On the first wave lifting the black prince into
view my son fired, but he took wing, and both of
us shot at him flying.   Kelly said he was hit,
and soon his prediction was verified—the little
bird rose in the air, wheeled, and fell dead in
the sea.

These being the only pair of black guillemots
seen, we were all (Kelly excepted) proportion-
ably elated.   The old whaler spun yarns about
seals, white bears, walruses, and other polar
wonders.   The sea-urchin whiffed his pipe and
grinned patronisingly.   Our skipper, however,
still peered stealthily to the west, and seemed
unwilling to lose time by a tack after a group of
eiders a little to the south.   We were now in no
mood to give in, so having settled that I was to
fire at the drakes and my son at the ducks, we
ran past them at long range.   He knocked over
his bird, and I struck mine, which flew a little

distance, and then dropped dead. The eider being also called the "St Cuthbert's Duck," we presented this case to my old and very dear friend, one of the ministers of St Cuthbert's. Of the former two cases — one is in my brother's collection at Rossdhu, the other in my own.

Under a rather stiff gale we recrossed the channel, but only when under the lee of the North Berwick coast did our captain's brow clear up. Well did this skilled boatman of the Firth know how suddenly the blast he had been dreading might, like Harpsdale's, come at last! With a quiet chuckle he muttered—"Noo we're a' richt," and joyously, not to say triumphantly, steered into port.

The death of the black guillemots on 7th April 1864 gave rise to the following correspondence:—

"THE BLACK GUILLEMOT.

" SIR,—The pleasantly-written articles upon the wild fowl of the Firth of Forth, with which your papers upon Natural History are agreeably begun, contain a statement, the importance of which the writer seems to have been unconscious of.

" In common, I believe, with every resident of
the neighbourhood of the Firth who has taken an
interest in its wild fowl, I am surprised to hear
that the black guillemot (*uria grylle*), the *Tyste* of
the Orcadians, is still to be met with in its waters ;
and I am yet more astonished to hear that its
nests are sometimes to be found upon the Isle of
May. Were it not that your contributor evidently
writes with a competent knowledge of marine
ornithology, I should at once consider that he has
mistaken young birds of the common guillemot in
their transition plumage for their black namesakes.

" There is no doubt that, if we can rely upon old
writers on natural history, the black guillemot did
at a former period build on the Bass, and, no
doubt, on the May, but I have never happened to
meet with any naturalist or sportsman who ever
found a single specimen in the Firth. As to their
nests, I am myself acquainted with almost every
nook and crevice of the Bass and May, and I think
I may absolutely say the black guillemot has
never been known to build on either within the
memory of man. They are found in vast numbers
among our more northern islands ; they are consi-

derably smaller than the razor-bill, and their nests are at once distinguished from others by the material fact that, like the little auk, they lay *two* eggs, whilst the rest of the species lay but one. The eggs, too, are considerably smaller, and much less pear-shaped than those of other rock-building auks.

"The common guillemot, the razor-bill, and the puffin, breed in the Firth of Forth, and the little auk is an occasional and most interesting winter visitor; but I confess I read with a doubting surprise that any other of the auk tribe has its nest on our islands.

"That stray specimens may sometimes appear, is not only a possible but a most probable circumstance; but that a gentleman should sail out with the intention of shooting black guillemots, and actually succeed in bagging two, will, I think, be looked upon by every local ornithologist as a most remarkable circumstance.—I am, &c.,

S."

The Author writes in reply to this communication: "I am delighted with your correspondent

'S.'s' letter. Sanderson, the bird-stuffer, of 66 George Street, knows I went to the May for the express purpose of shooting a black guillemot. He stuffed the two for me when I returned. Kelly, of North Berwick (the fisherman), his father-in-law, and a lad in his boat, saw my son and me shoot them exactly as described, and I refer 'S.' to both these parties. Lastly, the pair is stuffed and placed in my case of rock birds at my house, No. 1 Royal Terrace, where I invite 'S.' to go and inspect them. One is jet black, the other speckled. Both were shot the same day of April 1864. I have not my journal by me of last year, or I could tell the day. It is in Edinburgh, at my house there."

DEER-DRIVING IN MULL.

" Hunts he Bentalla's nimble deer."

DEER of the woods, although often large and heavy, are seldom gifted with what foresters call " a good head." The cover of trees is unfavourable to that branching development of the horns which a life on the open hills seems more fitted to foster. As " heath-covered Mull" is entirely grazed by sheep, its deer feed chiefly in the tangled woods and copses, and are loath to show themselves on the bare hill, where they may be chased by a collie dog, or "potted" by its master's "swan post," with no witnesses to the murder but the " wild flock," the eagle, or the raven.

I was tenant of two good deer drives in Mull, distant about ten miles from each other, Bentalla,

C

the faithless "Lord of the Isles'" hunting-ground, rising between. The Scalastal range on "the Sound" contained two large woods. One of them, however, called Garmony, had been lately cut, and was next to useless. But the Scalastal wood, when the wind was in the right direction, generally harboured some old deer. To keep all quiet, I also rented Scalastal farm and farm-house, turning my shepherds into game-preservers, and training their sheep-dogs to run the deer.

Glenforsa, the other shooting quarter, was situated on the opposite side of the island. In addition to some smaller patches, there were the fine hillside coverts of Garrochree and Torlochan—the former as wild a jungle as even this rugged island could grow. When either of these shootings was driven, especially if the deer were much frightened and the wind favourable, they were apt to cross Bentalla to the other. So, after a hunt at Scalastal, we were not unlikely to find the same deer next day at Glenforsa, and *vice versa*.

Like many tenants of deer, we were limited on both shootings. Three harts and two hinds was the Glenforsa allowance. A like number of hinds on Scalastal, but they were not so strict about the harts. These restrictions seldom annoy the man who kills his full complement, but they are most disgusting to a party who, at the close of a season, are far below the figure it was thus plainly intimated they were *expected* to slay. My predecessor, although assisted by his keeper and other guns, did not kill one deer among them the whole season. I also knew a party in the north, limited to seventy-five harts, end the season with fifteen, and in the shooting of this small lot they were aided by the resident foresters.

The first year of my Glenforsa lease I had only a few days at its deer. Our first stag was killed by my son when I was in England. I had charged him not to disturb the Glenforsa deer until my return, and he had kept strictly to small game at Scalastal. Two days before I was expected in Mull he drove over to Glenforsa House, with my Scalastal farm overseer, to prepare for our hunt. On the low ground along the banks of Loch-na-Gaul, with the river Knock flowing through it, is a detached strip of plantation much liked by deer, and, if undisturbed, seldom without them. When moved they have three escapes from this wood. When they break at the south corner and make for Garrochree, two of these escapes are guarded by the Knock pass. But should they seek safety in Torlochan wood, they slip out from the middle of the plantation, running east over a bare field, at the top of which, under cover of a drain, is placed the rifle. The Knock pass is far the most certain, not only as commanding two escapes, but also from being more used by the deer.

On the second afternoon my son, having completed his arrangements, agreed with the manager, that as the deer would be nearly certain to break cover at the Knock pass, there could be no harm in giving this patch an afternoon trial. Of the two chances commanded by the Knock pass, one is exactly 120 yards, the other about 30. It is impossible to equalise the distances without sacrificing one of the chances.

Yarrow's shrill yelp in the plantation soon warned my son that the manager had found deer. A large stag broke on the lower side of the river, came softly round the knolls, and made for the 120 yards pass. Here he had to cross the water, but seemed in no hurry to wet his feet. The collie had not yet left the wood, and the hart listened and watched to see when he did. All this time, the deer being in a slanting posture, my son refrained from firing, well aware that the moment he attempted to ford he must present a fair broadside. Black Yarrow now flitted from the covert, and the stag cautiously waded into the stream. Crack goes the rifle, down came the deer on his knees—recovered, and began to hobble across the current. A shot from the second barrel and he toppled over in mid-stream.

The first act after killing a deer is to examine where the ball has hit him. This time, there were two marks through the brisket, on the opposite side to the shooter, but only one on the near side; it was therefore apparent that both balls had entered at the same hole. Considering the distance, this was therefore a beautiful right and left rifle shot. The weight of this deer was 18 stone, and he had a very good head for Mull. I was much pleased with this auspicious start; the more

so as the manager saw more deer in the wood,
which he had refrained from disturbing.

Dogs thoroughly trained to drive deer coverts,
even when running a hot scent, should be taught
immediately to quit it, and return to their master
at his whistle. The reason is obvious. When
the deer are through the passes, further pursuit by
a dog only tires *him* and scares the deer further
away. As soon therefore as the quarry before
them are past the rifles, the dogs should be called
back into the covert to find a fresh track. Often
a stray hart or hind turns back by facing the
drivers, and remains quietly hid until the wood is
searched a second time. An old Mull collie,
which once aided our drive, was so knowing, that
of his own accord he returned to his master whenever the deer had escaped the shooters. This
sagacious creature knew every ambush guarding
the wood, and as soon as the deer were out of
danger, quite comprehended that it was useless to
follow where there were no rifles to kill.

Our cover pack consisted of two pure-bred Mull
collies, and a mongrel sheep-dog, which looked
like a cross between the old Scotch cur and a

jackal. The island pair were *mis*-named Trim and
Yarrow by their Tweedside master (my farm
grieve), but the nondescript was more aptly styled
" the Ugly Buck." He was a cross-grained, eccentric, unsociable, surly brute—had to have his teeth
broken for biting the sheep—would follow or obey
no one but his shepherd master, and when fairly
" blooded" at deer, considered himself discharged
from the meaner duties of sheep. Although Trim
and Yarrow had good noses, and stuck well to their
track, yet somehow I always felt most certain of
a shot when the covert rang with the wolf-like
howl of the Ugly Buck.

The day after my landing in Mull was pour-
ing rain, but the following brightened up again.
Scarcely expecting above one chance, I only put
four bullets in my pocket, and took a single-barrel
seal-rifle, which fitted me exactly.

The manager, his two Mull shepherds, and their
three dogs, were sent to the far end of the Knock
plantation, while I guarded the Knock pass, and
my son watched the other escape to Torlochan
wood. The dogs had hardly been thrown into
covert when they opened full cry. I distinctly

heard the hunt begin at the north end, and gradually near the south of the plantation. Soon
two hinds broke below the river, but instead of
making for the ford of the Knock, and giving me
the 120-yard chance, they kept the open shore of
Loch-na-Gaul, and, *contrary to all precedent,* took
refuge on the hills of Knock.

I was testily watching their wilful course, when
I heard a step approaching on the *near* side of the
river.   In a moment I knew it to be a deer's.   A
dip in the ground concealed the tramper until a
pair of horns rose about 30 yards from my hiding.
A fairer chance there could not be.   He crossed at a
trot, and I shot him through the heart.   My son
from his pass had noted this hart the moment he
quitted the wood—had marked him confidingly
choose his way straight for my hiding-place—was
well aware that I could not see him until he came
slap upon me—and, to crown all, perceived my
attention fixed on the hinds.   The thrilling suspense did not cease until he saw me present my
rifle.   This deer weighed 15 stone, but had a poor
head.

The overseer assured us there were two more

hinds in the wood, which had "turned back." To give my son *his* turn, we exchanged passes, but fortune again favoured me: the hinds broke at the wood-side for Torlochan, came up the field, and cantered past me at about 60 yards. I rolled over the largest, and if my rifle had been a double-barrel, had an easier chance at her companion.

We now had to choose our stances for a beat of the large hill-wood of Torlochan. Again the most likely pass was awarded to my son, while I chose mine by the side of a detached rock called "the Rock pass." This extensive covert requires to be searched with great care and labour. I heard the shouts of the men—now up the hill, now down, then across—until I was quite tired out; not a deer seemed to be in the wood. All of a sudden our pack struck up a jarring chorus. At first the chase bore for my son's ambush, but passing it out of range, made for mine. A hind soon showed herself about 100 yards off. I used my rock for a rest and fired; the deer staggered, then slowly walked towards me. When within 40 yards she halted—a lovely chance. Of course I began to load the single barrel. She listened for a moment, then slunk behind the adjoining heights. Taking a circuit for the wind, I came round them, and was expecting every instant to come upon the wounded deer, when a fresh pair of hinds turned up at long range on the open heath. Putting up the 200-yard sight, I fired the last of my balls! I saw it miss the deer and strike the hill about a foot before them. After loading with powder, I put my hand into my pocket for the bullet!! Here was a fix—for within 100 yards of where I threw away my last ball stood the stricken hind. She allowed me to walk within the fairest range, then limped down the hill, taking refuge in the thickets of Garrochree. It was more than an hour ere I could collect my men and dogs, but by that time the scent had cooled, not even the Ugly Buck deigning to notice it. We searched till dusk, by which time I had come to the conclusion that it is less troublesome to take too many bullets than too few.

THE GARROCHREE STAG.

He was a lonely one, caring nothing for company, large, intensely cunning, and carrying a

royal head. From his partiality to the impervious whins of Garrochree he had gained his
title. He never willingly left his fastness, except
when the flies forced him, returning to it whenever the July sun had abated his fierceness.
When hunted he ran a ring round and round the
thickest underwood, avoiding every open, and
confounding the dogs by the labyrinth of his
traces. I have known him dodge about in this
manner for half a day, and yet never be once
seen either by sportsmen or beaters. The well-
known " catch a weasel asleep " might well have
been applied to him ; and yet this big weasel *had*
been caught napping, but for breaking the pro-
verb nearly paid the forfeit of his life.

A former tenant of Glenforsa had an eight-
barrelled rifle, with which he used to astonish
the Mull natives by breaking bottles at fabulous distances, and no doubt he was a crack rifleman — *at the target.* One calm summer day,
soon after his taking possession, a wood-cutter,
in passing through Garrochree wood, spied a
pair of antlers peering out above the low whins.
Shrewdly suspecting the owner of the horns could

not be far off, the man of the axe went to
Glenforsa house and apprised Mr —— of his
discovery. The eight barrels were soon shotted,
and the rifleman, guided by the woodman and
accompanied by the farm-grieve (who told me
the above particulars), was soon close to the
stag's lair. The rifleman was perfectly concealed,
and to increase his chances of success the deer
had risen, and, all unconscious of peril, was crop-
ping the rich grass within point blank range.
The eight barrels were levelled; barrel 1, the
stag started; barrel 2, looked about to see where
the noise came from; barrel 3, walked a few
paces, and then listened; barrel 4, shook his
head and looked towards the enemy; barrel 5,
the stag, like a determined duellist, having accepted five shots, thought he had done enough
to prove his courage, and resolved never to stand
fire again.

Our men and dogs having been quite done up
by severe work, we gave them a day's rest, to
enable them to do justice to our last deer-hunt
of the season. But the wind was "wrong" for
our final day. No deer consequently in Knock

wood—not a track in Torlochan—the evening
fast closing in, and our only hope the rugged
jungle of Garrochree. To humour the wind and
command a view of the hunt, we occupied the
high passes, but after the morning failures had
about equal hope of moving a rhinoceros as a
red-deer. I was listlessly looking at the men
taking ground ere they threw the dogs into the
thicket, when my eye picked up a deer slowly
threading a devious course, but evidently making
for the open hill. With keen interest I watched
its many wayward angles and wheels, when suddenly halting and casting a glance at the baffled
dogs and men, it stalked into the bare ground—a
majestic royal stag. Choosing the pass immediately beyond those where we were concealed, and
bringing his noble profile into full relief against
the evening sky, he disappeared leisurely over
the ridge of the hill. This was the first time I
saw "the Garrochree stag," but it was not the
last.

Our second Mull season began as prosperously
as the first, but we had the advantage of another
gun, both my sons having got a fortnight's leave

from their regiments.   Before settling to regular
work, the "green hand" had the honour of drawing first blood, by killing a hart of 14 stone, at a
scrambling afternoon beat of Torlochan wood.   It
was a snap in the thick of the trees with an
S.S.G. cartridge, and the only shot fired that
day.

Our plan was to give several days first to
Scalastal, reserving the last week for Glenforsa,
as a *bonne bouche.*

It was the first week of October, and the stags
had given notice by some trumpet-blasts that the
season of warfare was at hand.   The Scalastal
overseer told us they came down after nightfall to
feed on a field of turnips close to the farm-house,
and one of them for the last few nights had been
"roaring like mad."   I was seated by a good fire
reading, when the man popped in his head to say,
that the stag was "at it again," and urging me to
come out and hear his defiant music.   The sudden
change from the bright and comfortable glare of
the fire and candles to the solemn gloom of a
moonless and starless night, whose silence was
only broken by occasional bellowings of the stag,

suggested to one's fancy an Indian prairie or African desert rather than one of our own Hebrides covered with its brown heath and shaggy wood.

When the grieve thought my mettle was up for a shot, he slyly observed that a fowling-piece loaded with buck-shot *might* hit them even in so dark a night, and felt confident that he could grope his way to the gap in the wall where the deer entered to " *spoil!* the neeps," and by which they also retreated when satisfied. To prevent them getting our wind, we had to make a considerable circuit through rough hill ground, to clamber over a high fence, and, worst of all, to cross Scalastal brook. Had I not been confident the man could find his way blindfold, I should certainly have declined the whole thing. No sooner had we quitted the outer door into the black still darkness, than I felt powerless as a child. The overseer, however, was alert enough. First tracing a sheep-path to guide him to the fence, which he followed down until he discovered the rude steps he sought, then listening for the brook, he rather anxiously whispered, "If we

were but through the burn," and led the way.
The burn was full of large stones, deep linns, and
swollen by recent rain ; but by finding the ford
we managed to scramble through, about knee-
deep. Guided by the bellowing of the deer (for
we now distinguished more than one roaring), the
gap in the turnip field was easily found, and I
was quickly squatted, so as to have the quarry
between me and the sky when steadying themselves for the leap down from the field into the
moor. My sons and the shepherds had to move
them from the lower end, where they were now
feeding, and when they reached the gap they
would be about ten paces from my ambush. A
few minutes of suspense, and we heard the rush
of the deer bounding in our direction. They
halted with only the wall between us. Every
moment I expected a dark figure on the sky-line,
but they seemed bent on trying our patience.
Only when the drivers were close on them did
they deign to move, and then, instead of their
convenient egress, wandered alongside the wall
and made an uncomfortable exit at the burn !
The wind being all right, it was impossible they

could either have smelt, seen, or heard us, and we could only account for the mishap by that caprice common to all living creatures as well as deer. When groping our way home, we consoled ourselves by the hope that we should certainly find these same harts next day in Scalastal wood.

When the wind is north, the south passes of course guard the extensive oak copse of Scalastal. They are four in number, nearly in line. As the wood hangs on a hillside, the passes rise one above the other, and were known to us as the high pass, the middle pass, the low pass, and the lowest pass. Attended by the grieve, to point out the ground, we scaled the hill, directing the shepherds to allow us twenty minutes law, before throwing the dogs into the low side copsewood flanked by the burn. I preferred the middle pass (*medio tut. &c.*), my eldest son the high one (*excelsior*), his brother the highest he could get! and the lowest was left to itself and *the deer*.

Both my sons had taken their ground, but the overseer was in the act of pointing out mine, when the lugubrious tones of the Ugly Buck swelled out in the wood close beneath. In an instant a hart burst from the thicket, and ran past at a sling gallop. "Noo, sir," from behind me—certainly a thoughtless hint, which has coaxed many a young sportsman into a dead miss. Fortunately, in this instance, the shooter was old and callous, so he took his time, and the hart fell dead in the heather. "Look oot, sir, for anither." The second warning fully atoned for the first. It was scarcely given when another hart galloped fair across our path, and he also rolled head over heels on the hillside. My favourite "Henry" rifle was loaded again in a twinkling, but no more deer turned out, neither did any try my sons' ground; but we heard from a neighbouring shepherd that a third hart had sneaked out at the *rejected* pass. The two killed were exactly the same weight, 15 stone, and both were shot through the shoulder, galloping, at 70 yards' distance.

The turnip field was quiet enough to-night, and not a roar heard far or near. Suspecting that "the lowest pass" fugitive would return in the night to Scalastal wood in search of his brethren, we arranged another drive for next morning. At this hunt our posts were the same, except that my second son was now convinced that it is sometimes good policy to choose the lowest place. The dogs soon found a hot track, but the run was long, and the deer stubborn. For nearly two hours they stuck to the scent, threading their nimble quarry round every rugged knoll and through many a tangled thicket. At last, when least expected, and the cry of the dogs at the furthest point of the covert, the object of their pursuit, in the shape of an old hind, quietly stole out of the wood, and stood opposite me, listening—a fine broadside, though rather distant chance. I fired, and struck her hard. She turned again for hiding to the copse, but a shot from the second barrel brought her down. There were no more deer found all day, so the hart had not returned.

Our last Scalastal day was intended for black game and grouse, and as the cutting of Garmony wood (which had spoilt it for deer) made fine open shooting at black game, we gave it the first trial. Our bags were fast filling with young blackcocks, and old ones too, before we got to the further end of the wood, where the moor-ground of Garmony and Fishness begins. Here we meant to range for

grouse, but, to our surprise, a deer was watching
our motions on this open moor, distant about half-
a-mile. As it was a very small hind, we thought
the No. 5, *if near enough*, might possibly add her
to the game list of the day. Leaving my youngest
son at the spot where the deer was likely to enter
the wood, and sending my eldest round the knolls,
to take post a little way above her, I coupled up
our brace of setters, making them and the retriever
follow me. The attention of the deer was at once
fixed on me and my dogs. She never took her eye
from us until, having got fairly in her rear, I
began to whistle and draw up. As I hoped, she
went away at a walk, looking now and then over
her shoulder to see if she was pursued. The
marksman above had thus ample time to shift his
ground, so as to meet her at the nearest point
among the heights. She never detected the ambuscade until within 40 yards, when she was saluted
by a right and left. Starting off at speed, she
made straight for the other gun, but the rough
ground soon hid her, until we heard a single shot.
Glad that it was not a *double* one, we hurried up
to see the sportsman triumphantly seated on his

quarry. It was only a yearling, and had been
fairly hit by the double shot, some of the pellets
we picked out of the hair not having even pene-
trated the hide. The single shot was only about
10 yards off, and killed her on the spot.

Early next morning our " 'bus " was at the
door for Glenforsa. This massive equipage had
a railed roof strong enough to bear a ton, im-
movable windows, and a low door at the stern,
usually strapped open. We yoked the heaviest of
the farm horses as wheeler, and in the lead an old
white Mull garron of twenty-five, harnessed with
cart ropes, and ridden by the lightest shepherd
as postilion. When the top was loaded with
provisions, and the inside filled by sportsmen,
dogs, and rifles, with the overseer as state coach-
man, we grinded slowly but merrily along to the
wonder and amusement of Mull residents.

The wind had not been in " the richt Glenforsa
airt " for some days, so of course there were
few deer on the ground. Our first hunt was
thoroughly unsuccessful. Only one hind in " the
Knock," which bounded past me out of all fair
distance for Torlochan wood. I put up the long

sight, and missed with both barrels. We were now sure of at least one deer in Torlochan, and as usual took post to guard the runs from this wood to Garrochree. The highest Torlochan pass, which I chose, commands a fine view of Garrochree, so I was nearly certain to detect deer leaving either wood. The dogs soon found the hind in Torlochan, and chased her round the wood, when she bolted through an unguarded pass into Garrochree. Trim and Yarrow followed in company, and I was tracing their course, and trying to make out the quarry among the trees, when full before me, and within a short distance of his first escape, stood the Garrochree stag. Well aware that the dogs were not after him, he was complacently watching the hunt, and when he saw his territory fairly invaded retreated through his customary defile. I looked revengefully at his exit, and hoped to come round him yet. With the exception of these two deer, all our coverts were drawn blank, and after a hard day's work we returned to Glenforsa House—cheered, however, by a change of the wind.

The customary rest-day was given to the pack,

which we devoted to the Glenforsa pheasants, killing the round dozen, besides hares and rabbits. As the wind had continued steady, we felt sure of deer next day, and in walking home were concerting the best mode of driving the covers, when the overseer met us with dejected mien. "The Ugly Buck has bolted after his master to Scalastal," says he. "We cheated him a' day that Dugald was here, but the naasty beast fan' us oot and set after him." To supply the place of the truant we asked a day's driving from the shepherd who owned the old dog already referred to, which was at once cheerfully given.

Maclean and his collie walked up the avenue next morning—just such a study as would have charmed the eye and inspired the pencil of our late unrivalled Wilkie. He was a tall, broad-shouldered, handsome young man, with black curly hair streaming under the blue bonnet, a shepherd's crook in his hand, and that peculiar shamble which proved at once that the roads were his detestation, and the hills his delight. His dog, known as the best in Mull, would not have been tolerated among the useless showy creatures that generally take first prizes at dog exhibitions, for it required a thorough sportsman to appreciate his points. Low in size and stiff in gait, his limbs slightly curved, and his hair wiry—at a passing glance most people would have called him ugly; but the broad chest, the round firm foot, the breadth of the head between the ears, and the exceeding intelligence and mildness of the eye, would soon have arrested the attention of a real judge of canine merit to the exclusion of all other fanciful points of useless beauty.

Wishing to take full service out of the man and his dog, we set him to the large rough woods of Torlochan and Garrochree first, reserving "the Knock" for the evening, if we had time. After giving strict injunctions to the grieve not to allow his dogs to break into Garrochree again, I chose the lowest pass, where the hind eluded us before. The chance is generally a long-running one, but open and broadside. The dogs found at once, and stuck to their game beautifully. Several times the deer came close to my pass, then seemed to lose heart when facing the open, and returned to the shelter of Torlochan. There was a larch plantation close to me, by which deer might have skulked into Garrochree, but it was so near to the cultivated ground that they were afraid to try it. Yet, after several times shirking her "beaten path," the hunted deer bounded down this wood within 40 yards of the bush where I lay in wait. The shot was so quick as to be *almost* a snap : she darted forward like the wind. My left barrel was so arrant a snap that I never saw the deer drop. After despatching her with my knife, I found my first ball had passed through her entrails, and the second broken both her hind legs. Had it not been for this last fortunate chance, she might possibly have escaped for the present, although certain to die soon after in the woods.

Before disturbing Garrochree, we went by the side of Loch Baa to a small lonely oak copse, where a good hart had harboured all summer. My pass was again the low one, and by lying flat I had the benefit of a fine rest for the rifle. No sooner into covert than the pack opened, and in a short time I spied the stag's horns coming out of the wood. It was an enviable chance—fair, open, slow, and broadside. It *would* have been a bungle had he not dropt to shot. Weight, 17 stone, and a very good head.

Now for the Garrochree stag! "We know his tricks—only let him try them," was the boast of our party when marching to rouse the doomed monster. His retreat was securely barred by my eldest son, while I took my former vantage-ground to give notice of his approach by a wave of my cap. He was at home as usual, but no persuasion could force him from his fastness. In vain Maclean's dog found him several times hid in an impenetrable thicket: he always ran the ring of the jungle, and then clapping suddenly down, was lost until he was rested for another race. I never ceased watching the old collie, and never saw such endurance and pluck shown by any dog that ran the foot. Sticking to his track like a bloodhound, not once overrunning it, or slacking his pace, facing briars and whins that appalled the other dogs, and all the time attending to the slightest signal of his master, he proved himself nobly possessed of intelligence, perseverance, and self-command, qualities which have always been the making of great *men!*

Returning home jaded enough by a hard day, yet pleased with its success, we were welcomed by the Ugly Buck and his master, just arrived from Scalastal. As we dared not part them again, we despatched the pair in the fishing coble to bring home the hart—the hind lay within a few hundred yards of the house.

A Scotch mist was a good excuse for declining the hills next morning, and as there were only two more days before the steamboat touched at our island, the dogs would be nicely rested for the concluding hunt. It was a lovely one that last day in Mull, bright, calm, and bracing enough to inspirit a clod. Of course, the first point to prove was whether *the* stag would try skulking tactics. A short cut led me to the look-out on the hill, but my son had to go round with the beaters and ascend the high ground from behind, so as to humour the wind and reach his ambush unobserved. I saw him breasting the hill and nearly on its crest, when one of the shepherds thoughtlessly called to the dogs. It was a low caution, yet was distinctly heard by me through the thin air, and of course by the wily deer. As the rifle-

man, however, was now on the hill-top, and rapidly
descending to his post, all seemed safe, when at
this critical moment, and never suspecting that an
enemy was marching parallel and would soon be
in possession of the defile, quietly emerged from
the thicket the object of our wiles. Scarcely able
to restrain my impatience, I yet felt sure that a
" haste signal" would put the stag on his guard;
but if left to his own devices, he might possibly
linger until retreat was death. The marksman,
equally unconscious of the magnificent trophy
almost within reach of his rifle, stepped briskly
on, and was within rifle shot of the pass when the
deer glided carelessly into it. Had he been aware
of the position of his victim, even now the stag
could not have escaped; but by inadvertently
crossing his wind the danger was instantly revealed. Raising his branching front, and snuffing the
" tainted gale," he vanished suddenly round the
hill, and with him all hope of adding to our list
the royal head of the Garrochree stag.

As there were no more deer in Garrochree, the
hunt was sent round to the north end of Torlochan
to beat up for the south passes, which we had now

to guard. My son having chosen the low pass, where the last hind fell, I had simply to face about, and walk a few forward paces to command the high runs. A view of the distant sea, flanked by its noble range of mountains, with the silvery Loch Baa at my feet, had pretty well lulled my vigilance, when a single shot from below roused me from my reverie. The three dogs soon after swept through the low pass full cry, and, skirting the shores of the loch, seemed making for the rough cover of Garrochree. Although nearly a mile above, I saw a small object take the water and strike out for the opposite side. Fixing the telescope, I felt satisfied that the noise had scared a sheep (no unfrequent result) from the low banks into Loch Baa for safety. It had nearly gained mid-loch when I heard the rapid stroke of oars, and presently the fishing-coble, pulled by the shepherds at their utmost stretch, headed back the swimmer in the direction from which it had started. I now distinctly traced two animals in the water, and their pursuer running to meet them at the salmon-point, where they seemed bent on landing. He fired, and missed the head of one, which wheeled about and swam for another point, but its companion struck ground and fell dead to the second barrel. The boatmen quickly took the sportsman on board, and ere the first he fired at could gain the shore he shot her through the head. The pair, an old hind and her calf, were the only deer in Torlochan wood, and the marksman being *now* in no humour to throw away a chance, had hit the hind through the back running, at 130 yards, when she took the water, followed by her calf. The latter was fortunately a male, so we had exactly completed our year's lot of three harts and two hinds.

A CONTRETEMPS.

I shall conclude these wood-driving reminiscences of Mull by a deer-stalking incident at my next shooting quarter, which, as "a comedy of errors," was quite unique.

Accompanied by a friend and my second son, we were returning from fishing the high pools of the Falloch, when the hill-watcher met us in hot haste with the welcome news that a couple of harts were feeding in a wild corrie of the Arnan, and he did not think they were likely to be disturbed, or quit their ground for some time.

Leaving our friend and the keeper to finish the lower waters of the river, my son and I made short work of exchanging rods for rifles, and were soon at the base of the Arnan hill. The watcher's face grew long, for the deer had shifted, and although we were all right as to the wind, yet a slight movement among any of the numerous sheep feeding all round might instantly put them on their guard.

Peter Robertson, of "the Black Mount," had kindly lent us a very good lurcher for bringing wounded deer to bay, yclept Friday, whose black coat was another source of anxiety. Sending the man forward with a telescope, we squatted down with the lurcher behind a bank, determined to wait patiently till our spy was thoroughly satisfied. In about half-an-hour he returned, his radiant visage, even before he spoke, showing all was right. The harts, he told us, were resting on a height some way off, but by humouring the ground I soon got a capital view of them. They might be approached from below or from above, but I always like the high stalk best, as deer are so much less apt to

look up than down hill. In this instance the
watcher was clearly for the low approach, as he
feared our deerhound might scare the sheep, scattered thickly over the heights. Notwithstanding,
I decided to risk it, and by *stalking* the sheep and
screening the dog among us, we at last got safely
beyond them. The harts were now close at hand ;
so leaving the watcher with Friday on the leash,
we were soon at the back of the knoll, where we
had seen them lying. I directed my son to keep
about eighty yards above me, lest they might have
risen, and separated, but not to show himself until
I had fired.

On looking through a tuft of heather, I saw
the deer on their legs—fine side chances—the
largest about 50, and the other fully 100 yards
off. I fired a double shot; and my son called
down, "You've done for them both." The near
one ran a short way and fell dead, but the other,
dropping on its knees, rolled over the opposite
side of the height, on the crest of which it was
standing, and limped down the hill until close to
my son, where it halted, staring at him within
pistol-range. At this moment, a third hart gal-

loped across the face of the corrie, which I mistook for the wounded one, and called to the watcher to slip the dog. There was a beautiful course, Friday turning the deer whenever he tried the steep, but down-hill the hart had the best of it. Expecting soon to be warned by the bay that our fugitive was " at a standstill," we all followed in pursuit; but when poor Friday returned chopfallen and bloodless, our disappointment was extreme. " At any rate, one of them is safe," says the younger sportsman. " I should think so," rejoined the elder, " when I measured his head!" " Measured his head! why, he came *to me*, his leg swinging like a flail, and stood about fifteen paces off. I could almost have knocked him down with the butt of the rifle." " I saw the deer dead enough in the heather; and if the Captain saw anither, there must have been three," put in the watcher. " Well," says the first speaker, " if there is one lying dead, you are sure enough of the wounded one, for he couldn't outrun a man, far less a dog. I only didn't fire because I felt sure I could walk up to him."

Friday had, however, taken us two long *hill*

miles from the spot, and fully an hour and a half
had passed since the chase began. When we got
to the place where the wounded hart stood, he
was nowhere to be seen. We sought the hill till
evening, but the ground was very rough, and
covered with the longest heather, also full of deep
holes. Next day the search was renewed with
additional dogs and men, but without finding any
traces of the stricken hart. Since this series of
stalking blunders, I have always recommended
young deer-stalkers to adopt the Kirkpatrick's
motto, " I will mak sicker."

WHEN salmon-fishing in the Tweed many years ago, with one of the most scientific *habitués* of that river, I casually asked him whether a late celebrated Professor was really so good a fisher as he got credit for? He answered, with a shrug, "Oh, he's only a trouter." Had this man been *only a salmoner*, a plain inference might be drawn; but he was undeniably as expert at small fish as large. Indeed, I cannot conceive an adept at salmon-fishing who has not laid the foundation by a thorough knowledge of all the best modes of capturing trout. For my own part, I began at six years old, with a crooked pin and worm, to dabble for minnows and loaches, being gradually promoted to a hook and float for perch-angling; then ascending to burn-trout with bait, which naturally led the way to burn-trout with fly.

Once fairly entered at fly, my progress was rapid. I soon became dissatisfied with my basket unless it contained some good ones; and, when large yellow trout in summer became shy of rising to artificial flies, changed the lure to minnows and other natural baits. At this time, too, I was a keen and successful pike-troller, and these fresh-water sharks first whetted my taste for really big fish. Having the advantage, however, of being near some fairish sea-trout streams, one autumn convinced me that the *salmo trutta* made the best sport of any fish I had yet tried. No doubt large, lazy, well-fed yellow trout were powerful rivals in spring, but they were only attainable with *bait* in autumn, when the reign of the white trout with *fly* began.

As I had opportunity, I tried a cast for grilse or salmon; but my knowledge of the habits of fish and my practice being alike limited, the rises were of course few and far between, so I always turned with increased zest to the fat yellow trout in May, or the silvery sea ones in September. It

was not until I was thoroughly acquainted with
the nature of fish, and had acquired perfect command of the salmon rod, that the intense excitement of hooking a 20-pounder tamed down my
interest for all minor angling.

With the exception of boat-fishing in strictly
preserved rivers, angling for large fish, in order to
reach the deep pools and heavy streams where
they lie, requires a length of line which few can
ever attain to throw. But when the river banks
are at the same time encumbered by trees or other
obstacles, the rods who can fish it well become
select indeed.   Of course the rises decrease in proportion to the want of power in reaching the casts ;
and the angler, however expert with a small rod
and fly, loses confidence when he looks over his
shoulder and sees a salmon struggling at his neighbour's line, hooked in the very pool he was unable
a few minutes before to cast over.   With the loss
of confidence his patience also deserts him, and he
returns to yellow trout, a stanch stickler for the
theory that trouting is the most scientific of all
fishing.   But if a man has thorough mastery of a
large rod, and quite comprehends the ways of the

noble fish he is trying for, also the various moods of water, sky, air, time of day, &c., when the monster may be most successfully lured, the crowning requisite, patience, always comes of its own accord.

In ordinary rivers the most expert angler well knows that he must not expect many rises of big fish; he therefore uses all his skill and experience to hook those he *does* move. This attention constantly increases his stock of knowledge, until he feels certain he can hook them if they *can* be hooked.

Where the rises are more numerous, there is not the same pains taken to profit by them; and this natural consequence partly explains what I have also noticed in shooting—viz., that a man who has lived among preserves, far from being so good a sportsman, is frequently not even to be compared as a steady shot with another whose whole practice is over wild unenclosed lands. The one blazes thoughtlessly away, committing time after time the same errors; while the other notes every miss, and endeavours to correct it next opportunity. There is also no doubt that both the angler and

shooter who have to work and *think* for their
sport, acquire a self-command and nerve only to
be obtained in this school.

Although loch and river fishing seem distinct
departments of the craft, yet the more closely they
are studied the nearer do they approximate to
each other. When white trout and salmon enter
a fresh loch, if there is no stream large enough to
ascend, they press to the mouths of the feeding
burns ; or should the loch itself be small, they
first choose (as in rivers) the feeding-grounds
farthest from the sea, those nearer gradually filling with " back fish." They have favourite rocks
and banks all over the loch, exactly as they have
favoured pools and streams in rivers. Lochs, as
well as rivers, are most successfully fished when
they fall after a heavy flood. In some places of a
loch, like some pools of a river, fish never rise well
at the fly, although the part of the loch and the
pool of the river may look very tempting to the
angler.

White trout and salmon creep down nearer the
outlet of a loch as autumn advances, preparatory
to choosing their spawning-beds. The top of a

small loch is therefore best early in the year, the
lower parts gradually improving as the season
draws on.   If, however, the feeders of a loch are
large enough for fish to ascend, their first object
is to seek them, and press up.   In the smaller
lochs the feeding burns may admit sea-trout
during floods, but are seldom large enough for
salmon ; the consequence is, that all the heavy
fish remain in the loch till harvest, and are very
apt to haunt the mouths of brooks during a spate.
This is the case even in Loch Lomond, where,
with the exception of the outlet (the Leven), there
is no stream where salmon dare enter, except at
the spawning-time; and it is amazing to see great
fish at that season in mountain brooks that will
scarce cover, far less conceal them.

   In Loch Awe, where the fine feeder Urchay is
ready to receive them, salmon seldom go up the
loch at all.   When clear of the river Awe (the
outlet of the loch), they immediately press on to
the Urchay, and enter it.   Consequently, salmon
are scarcely ever taken in the loch, except between the mouths of these rivers.

   When salmon know they have the safety of a

loch to look to as the reward of their efforts for fresh water, the struggle they hazard to gain their object is almost incredible. I have watched a shoal boring up the Knock for Loch Baa, when they had to turn on their sides to force themselves through the shallows, and the noise caused by these exertions could be heard at a considerable distance. At first I fancied some creature was fording the stream, and, on walking up, saw monsters of from 10 to 25 lb. fighting against water often only a few inches deep.

I have always been convinced that trolling is ruination to fly-fishing in small salmon lochs. All the shores, banks, and rocks have their feeding or resting fish driven into deep water, scared not only by the boat, but even by the long trolling lines sweeping over.

Fly-practice in lochs from a boat is far less startling to fish ; and the more complete the angler's knowledge of every sunk bank, rock, or shallow point, the less likely will he be to frighten them away. In order to obtain this angling geography, the loch should be surveyed in dry weather ; and when the different feeding-grounds are discovered, they should be noted by marks from different positions opposite to or crossing each other. A decayed stump of a tree exactly opposite a shepherd's hut, making a triangle with a rock or the end of a point, may be the only available beacons to guide you to a first-rate *mid-loch* cast. For two years I had the right to one side of Loch Baa, and by these simple means, before the first season was half over, knew all the established casts fully as well as the fishing guides, and found out some more they had no idea of.

Perfect confidence in this local knowledge is the foundation of success in lochs; and when the fisher fully possesses it, *and not till then*, will he perceive how many blunders he can prevent his boatman from committing. For instance, effectually to fish the feeding-grounds with the least risk of scaring them, it is absolutely necessary to know the exact spots where the salmon lie. When the feeding-ground has a sheer descent from shallow to deep water, this may be shrewdly guessed; but when the deep is reached gradually, a rise in the loch, or even a change of wind, may alter the seats of salmon a considerable way either side. As the angler's object is to keep his boat out of sight in deep water, and pitch his fly over the fish, when the water deepens suddenly from the bank or rock, he has simply to fish round them with a line longer or shorter, according to the state of the atmosphere or the power of the breeze. The salmon will all be found on or near the brow, and in a dark or windy day they do not see the boat until close on them. I have seen the heaviest fish rise and hook in such weather within a few yards of the boat—a rare chance for men who throw an indifferent line.

But should the day be clear, with only a light breeze, especially when casting over *shallow points and places where the water deepens by inches*, none but an accomplished master of the salmon-rod need hope for much success. Such ground must be approached with the greatest caution, or you may dash in among the shoal unawares. It is always best to err on the safe side, and begin to throw before you expect a rise, drawing in to the point where you think salmon really are by slow degrees.

Should the morning be favourable for fly, a little

attention to the rising of the fish will save both
time and trouble; but when the weather is not so
propitious, and, by consequence, few rises to be
seen, care and caution, far from wasting the day,
are the chief means of insuring success at its close.

There was a long promontory half-way down
Loch Baa, called "the Salmon Point," from being
their grand rendezvous. The area of the feeding-
ground extended to nearly 200 yards; and when
they were rising briskly, we could fish it over in
half the time required if they were dull and
sulky. This cape was one of the favoured haunts
where fish were sure to harbour all summer; and
even on the days when none were seen feeding on
the natural fly, you might depend on their resting
below—hence the need of always going carefully
over it. On two occasions, when wind and sky
were all that could be wished, I had carefully
gone over the Salmon Point without a rise, or
even seeing a fish stir at the natural fly. The
first time, when changing my cast for a fresh
trial, the head of an otter above the best part of
the water showed that my trouble would be useless. On the next unsuccessful day we were

resting on the shore after sweeping the water thoroughly; the otter's head again appeared, when he dived all round the fishing-ground, and finally landed, and ran into the wood. Other casts of this loch were more uncertain, the salmon and white trout often changing their ground. Here I may mention a rather unaccountable fact long noted by me—viz., that a cast of a loch or a pool in a river will sometimes prove excellent for a whole season, and during the next scarcely afford a rise, yet no outward alteration can be detected either in the loch cast or river pool.

The size and colour of salmon-flies do not vary nearly so much in lochs as in rivers. One reason no doubt is, that there are fewer changes in a loch; another, that the loch season is generally shorter. I have often found red palmers, or a red body with blae wing, very acceptable to salmon in small lochs; in large lochs a green body and darker wing is a killing fly; but every tolerable fisherman ought to be able to find out *the* fly of the water he frequents; and if a stranger, he must trust a good deal to his fishing guide. There is often a loch-fly, which, take the season from end

to end, you kill most heavy fish with; and yet
there are many whole days in the same year
when that fly will be rejected for another very
unlike it. Neither is it a necessary consequence
that the most killing fly of one year should be
also the most successful of the next. On the
contrary, I have experienced a complete change
in the favoured fly of the season, not only in
lochs, but in rivers.

The most deadly fly of the river Falloch altered
every season of the three years I rented it; and
although a large minnow was eagerly dashed at,
both by white trout and heavy loch ones which
ascended from Loch Lomond, yet I invariably
fixed all the largest sea-trout with fly and the
lightest tackle I dared risk. A grilse-rod and the
finest gut made a Falloch trout of from 4 to 7
pounds a good substitute for a 15 or 20-pound
salmon with ordinary tackle. The best Falloch
run I had was with a 4½-pounder hooked by the
belly fin. I had *almost* to swim before landing
him.*

* In the autumn of 1863, my last season on the Falloch, I
landed twenty trout of an aggregate weight of sixty pounds.

The heaviest Falloch sea-trout taken by me were from 5 to upwards of 7 lb.; but I have frequently captured them in Loch Baa from 9 to 12 lb. Like salmon, none of these Loch Baa monsters ever ascended the feeding burns, although in autumn one stream near the top of the loch was full of sea-trout from 1 to 3 lb. weight. My son, then a lad, used to row over to this mountain brook, and seldom returned without several of those white trout, besides a large basket of yellow. His last take was five sea-trout from 1½ to 3 lb., and seven dozen burn ones. He always fished with worm, and chose a day when the burn was quite dwindled. In such small water as this there was no need of a reel, but the gut required to be nearly as fine as horse-hair. As in burn-trout bait-fishing, he always threw up-stream, seldom, however, moving a sea-trout where the burn ones bit freely. These pigmies are obliged to keep their distance from the leviathans that invade them in autumn. Each sea-trout then chooses a pool, and preys easily and greedily in such clear confined water on the burn-trout fry, driving away those too large for food, in order to prevent them from sharing in the worms, slugs, &c., carried down the current. The little burn-trout are therefore compelled by fear, and the bigger ones by force, to desert the quarters of a dangerous and selfish usurper.

In loch-fishing, I have constantly observed that too much wind spoils sport more than too little, always excepting a dead calm. Salmon and white trout, however, will bear a stiffer gale than the yellow, at least if your boatman is expert at the oars, and perfectly knows the fishing-ground. If not, never take him out in a rough day, when you will find it impossible to make him obey your directions. A really efficient boatman is about as great a comfort as a thoroughly-trained retriever, and both contribute in no slight degree to the day's success. You may very soon teach for a fishing boatman an active and intelligent lad, but his first lessons should always be *learned in a calm.*

SEAL-SHOOTING.

"No man," says the old Highlander, "has any right to a hunter's badge who has not killed a red-deer, an eagle, a salmon, and a seal." Some also include the wild swan ; but this last test of Highland sportsmanship seems scarcely fair, as the hooper is a cosmopolitan bird of passage, frequenting in hard winters most of the undisturbed pieces of water in the United Kingdom. Although the lonely moor lochan is a favourite resort both of Bewick's and the common wild swan, there are also large tracts among our wildest mountain districts where they are never seen, or even heard of. I should, therefore, be inclined to reckon the hooper as a more correct criterion of skill in an

F

English fenman with mud boots and tarpaulins, than of a brogued and kilted Gael.

The killing of red-deer and salmon has been of late years so simplified by preservation, and by artificial modes of sporting, that even the Cockney who possesses the talisman (money) will very soon be made free both of the forest and the river. What would the ancient Hillman have thought of forests where the deer were nearly as tame as sheep, and so numerous as to be dwarfed both in size and antlers? With what contempt would he have growled his guttural at the sunk fences of the forest, and the boat-fishing of the Tay and the Tweed, when the pools and streams are so crowded with spring or autumn fish that the veriest green-horn could not escape hooking them!

This may be called the luxury of sport, but it is not the pleasure of it, for certainly our best pleasures must all be worked for and earned; at all events, these lazy and luxurious modes of deer and salmon murder were never contemplated by the Celt, who, in granting his diploma to a mountain hunter, deemed a single head of the famous four quite sufficient to entitle him to it.

Preserving, the chief means of bringing down to the level of almost any aspirant two of the four exploits required for a hunting degree, has, by driving it into remote fastnesses, made a third—viz., the death of an eagle—tolerably difficult to compass. As to the last on the list, the seal, let any one try to bag one under the most favourable auspices, and he may find the task less easy than it appears. I say "bag one" in place of shoot one, for most parties who have made the attempt with their rifles assure you they have been the death of many seals. On pressing the point, you are informed that they all sank on receiving the fatal bullet, and the defunct monsters are rotting under the waves.

For my own part—except those struck through the body on land—I have little faith in the death of seals thus suddenly submerged. When hit on land, if the shot is not a header, they are very likely to flounder into the sea and sink in deep water before you can possibly get hold of or trace them. But all swimming seals, if hit at all, are shot through the head, and immediately spread out on the surface, giving ample time to row up and seize a flipper. When the shooter has no boat, and does not possess the alternative of a large retriever dog, he should never fire at seals unless in places where, if killed, they can be recovered when the tide ebbs.

The sight of seals is not quick, but their other senses of scent and hearing are most acute. In stalking, either from land or water, they are more difficult of approach than deer; and in a calm day the creak or splash of an oar instantly puts the basking shoal on their guard, when they roll helter-skelter into the brine. As they can wind you at a mile's distance, coming on them to windward is out of the question; for on the scent warning that the enemy is dangerously near, they shuffle from the rocks into the safety of the deep. Although long aware of threatened danger, they are often too lethargic to fly until it really becomes imminent, but this laziness never tempts them to be so foolhardy as to risk their life.

A dead calm is, of course, best for seal-shooting from a boat, but a *favourable* breeze is an advantage, should the shoal be sunning themselves on the rocks; in which case, when afloat, always try to land and stalk from the shore. If from the direction of the wind or other obstacles this is impracticable, the shore chance from a boat is frequently an indifferent one, but the shot at the head when they come up after *the first dive* is almost certain to be point-blank.

A boat for seals should be light, and draw as little water as possible. For this purpose, and to prevent rocking, the build must be broad, short, and flat. Frequently you have to pole through shallows only a few inches deep, while now and then dragging your shallop over an isthmus may be the only means of securing an excellent chance. As dead seals always lie on their backs at the bottom, the white bellies may be seen at considerable depth. A strong cord with very large hooks and lead attached is, therefore, a most useful appendage to fish them up.

The monster ocean seals were rare in Loch-na-Gaul, but I have detected one or two about the entrance of the loch, always, however, shy of trusting themselves within bullet-range, and shunning the parts of the coast or the rocks where they might possibly be surprised. In the outer Hebrides these prodigious creatures are tame enough, and roam along the shores, the tyrants of these wild seas. I saw the skin of one, shot off the Colonsay coast by a nephew of the Lord Justice-General, which weighed 30 stone. It unexpectedly elevated half its body out of water, close to the young sportsman, when he shot it through the lungs.

One fine September day, when walking with a friend on the south shore of Loch-na-Gaul, fourteen Arctic seals came racing past close to land. They jumped and gambolled over each other like boys at leap-frog, making a splash in the sea that gave notice of their advent a good way off. After coursing some distance in this boisterous style they settled on a rock, and by stalking we got within rifle-range ; but not having a rifle, we were fain to content ourselves with a survey through the telescope—the first and last I ever had of these rare visitors from the Polar seas.

Even a quick eye requires practice ere it becomes expert at distinguishing basking seals on the rocks. They are so like tufts of seaware or detached stones, both in shape and colour, that the uninitiated may have a dozen ranged at no great distance, yet never perceive one. The smallest suspicious object, however, at once arrests the attention of an experienced seal-shooter, and he instantly fixes the glass to watch for a curve of the tail or a bend of the head. Like wildfowl and deer, when you detect the prey *before you are yourself perceived*, success is half attained; but this far sight and keenness of eye can only be arrived at by long use, and is one of the brightest feathers of the hunter's cap.

A reef of rocks near the head of Loch-na-Gaul, although completely submerged at high tide, begins to show itself at quarter ebb, and at low water they expand into considerable islets. This group is the favourite drying ground of seals in summer, and the nursery where they rear their young. Every calm, hot day, when the islets are left bare and quiet, the large heads of the female seals, each followed by a little head, oftener by a pair no bigger than cricket-balls, float about the tiny bays, while the old males sun themselves luxuriously on the shelving rocks. Whenever this dry sunny weather prevented salmon-fishing in Loch Baa, the

coble was carted from the fresh to the salt water
loch, and seals substituted for salmon.

After a sultry fortnight towards the end of June,
I noted with the telescope a flock of seals ranged
like sheep along the centre rock of the group. A
short time before, a new (Henry) rifle had been
forwarded; what an opportunity to handsel it!
The boatman was summoned, the rifle unpacked
and loaded, without even a pluff of powder to spoil
Mr Henry's "luck." A high rock of the nearest
islet, where I landed, screened us from the herd,
but they were beyond rifle-range, and no possibility of a closer approach. My tactics were soon
fixed. Taking post under a rock close to the sea,
I made the man unmuffle the oars, and, keeping
out of view, to pull away with as much noise and
bustle as he could. The success of this manœuvre
depended entirely on rousing the inquisitiveness
of the sleepers. No sooner was the sound of the
oars heard so near than the whole troop wriggled
into the water, and two of the largest sailed past
my rock at 80 yards' distance, peering curiously
round for a sight of the boat. Selecting the moment when his poll was my target, I fired, and

one of the monsters lay stretched on the sea. My
second barrel was ready for his companion, which
of course had dived, but *his* curiosity being satisfied, he never reappeared. The boatman obeyed
my signal at his utmost speed, and all but upset
the coble in dragging the seal on board. It was a
male, and weighed 9 stone.

The weather continuing calm and warm, the
same shoal a few days after settled on one of the
further rocks, but the look-out was too open to
permit our cheating them again, so there was nothing to be done but raise the long sight. I fired
at three in line, and must have hit a pair of them,
for we traced two tracks of blood to the sea, enter-
ing it from opposite sides of the rock. The surface was also covered with their fur, but the water
was far too deep to allow any hope of detecting
them at the bottom if dead.

The seals were now getting shy of these rocks,
but a burning day again enticed them to try a
siesta; this time, however, they cunningly chose
a bare exposure, *all but* safe from surprise. On
taking a survey with the telescope from the mainland, I arranged a plan by which we had a pros-

pect of getting within 150 yards, but the operation
was both difficult and tedious. By landing on
the outermost islet, and carrying the coble right
across into a creek dividing the first from the
second reef of rocks, we could pole down to the
shelter of a large stone, which might enable the
stalker, by a wet crawl among the seaweed, to
reach the distance I had calculated for a chance.
A crew of four was needed for the land transport
of our skiff, but to effect this *quietly* over slippery
rocks, although the turning-point of our strategy,
was its most trying part. The moist seaware
caused a few false steps among the rough rocks,
but its softness prevented these stumbles from
being heard by the seals, so the coble was safely
lodged in the creek. It was quickly pushed down
this latch, when I had to crawl flat a little way
among shingle and seaweed in order to reach the
nearest point for the shot.

After carefully noting the postures of the unsus-
picious but scattered flock, being unable to get two
in line, I put up the 150-yard sight and selected
one of the nearest. Instantly I saw and heard the
ball strike my mark true to the aim. Its com-

panions dashed into the sea, but the wounded seal rolled about on the sand, and then struggled after them. When in the water, in place of only the head, the whole disabled shoulder rose above the surface, and the dives were short and laborious. My boatmen, making sure of their prize, pulled with all their might, but in mid career an oar snapped, and there was no spare one. With the stump of the oar they followed the path of blood, and every time the creature came to the top for air the sea was dyed red all round. Had I and my rifle been aboard I could with the greatest ease have sent a ball through its head before the air supply was pumped out by the death-struggle, when it would have floated till we pulled up. Even with a pair of whole oars there was every likelihood of getting hold of the prey alive, but by lamely following it with an oar stump the creature bravely fought on till it died, and then, quite empty of buoyant air, disappeared at once in deep water. For the truthfulness of my narrative I have entered into these details, but must acknowledge that such casualties in seal-shooting fully counterbalance its pleasures.

The reaching of them when they felt so secure, and the smell of their comrades' blood, made the phoca troop shy of their rocks for some time. Before they again dared risk the pleasure of a bask, copious rain enticed us back to Loch Baa and the salmon, and it was the beginning of August ere I had another opportunity at seals.

The Garmony farmer had complained of a deer injuring his ripening crops, so to please him we came over to Scalastal for a range of Garmony wood. After an early breakfast the shepherds and dogs were sent forward to the further end of the covert, and I was loading my rifle and about to follow, when one of them ran back to tell us that a seal was resting on a submerged stone in the sound, opposite the farm gate. He had detained the deer hunt until he knew whether the rival claimant for the contents of my rifle would be first honoured. My son and the grieve went to reconnoitre, and reported that the seal was more than 200 yards from the gate. The stone was some 3 feet under water, and the creature, by resting its hind flippers on this platform, was standing upright in the sea, the head presenting even less of

a mark than if the seal had been actually swimming. It was impossible to get closer than the
gate, which, however, gave the advantage of a fine
rest.

I always like shooting ball at objects in water,
as a man is at once aware what kind of shot he
has made. In this instance I did not expect to hit,
but determined in the face of four witnesses to go
as near as possible to my aim. I never fired with
more deliberate calculation, but own I was nearly
as surprised as the onlookers when the animal
stretched on the surface dead. There was a rush
by the two fleetest of our party for the rickety
skiff, but long ere it was possible to pull round, I
had the mortification to see my prize turn on its
back and sink. I directed the rowers to the very
spot, but although there were two pairs of as sharp
eyes as ever scanned the deep, they could see
nothing white at the bottom. On coming into the
skiff I at once perceived that there was no possibility of detecting the object of our search, except
at the lowest ebb of the tide.

Our interrupted deer-hunt was again resumed,
but there being neither hoof nor horn to delay us

in Garmony wood, we had plenty time to be at the seal again by the turn of the tide. After launching the skiff and placing a shepherd to direct our course from the shore, my son, the grieve, and I endeavoured to find the resting-stone, now confounded with several others ; but an unfortunate breeze so obscured and hindered the search, that we had gone round and over the white mark three times before my son called out, " I see him." With difficulty backing the boat so as to keep sight of the creature for the few seconds required to cast off my coat and shoes, I plunged into the sea, and at the first dive caught hold of the hind flippers and raised it to the boat-side. Had we been provided with our seal-grappling apparatus (left at Glenforsa), from the roughness of the water and the strength of the wind, the task would have been both more lengthy and precarious. This seal was a female between 7 and 8 stones weight.

Late in the season, when the colder days had thinned the Loch-na-Gaul rocks of their floundering visitants, my eldest son, who had been absent all the seal season, and was anxious to bag one, had the fishing-coble again transplanted for a day

or two from Loch Baa to the salt water. He took
post on one of the islets, and in orthodox style,
Hythe position, hit his game fair through the
head, swimming fully 100 yards off. This seal,
however, did not require either a dive or the grap-
pling-hooks, as I managed to get hold of and drag
it into the skiff before it settled and sank.

A RATHER curious speculation has sometimes amused me. Had rare old Gilbert White been a sportsman instead of a naturalist only, and had he rented grouse muirs, should we have gained or lost most by his metamorphosis ? No doubt 'Selborne,' the most charming and classic of sketches, might have been less perfectly filled up ; but, on the other hand, if the keen and philosophic eye of this magic painter caught but a passing glimpse of what hundreds regard no more than the "idle wind," what curious theories might have been started, and in what beautiful language would they have been handed down !

Power of pitching his tent in the remote wilds, and of removing it as his fancy may prompt, is

the great boon given to the sportsman-naturalist
by the present universal system of leasing shoot-
ing-ground. A goodly number of our keenest and
best sportsmen are naturalists also, and when to
this accomplishment is added an enthusiastic love
of scenery, their enjoyments are greatly enhanced.
For the last thirty-two years I have been one of
these autumnal wanderers, and rented shootings
not only in the north, south, east, and west of
Scotland, but also in the islands, thus having the
opportunity of comparing different districts of the
country, and noting, by the effects of climate, &c.,
on its various fauna, the slight causes which
often diverge into wide results.

My present abode, the romantic old Castle of
Kames in Bute, has supplied me with a fresh field
of amusement and research in the study of that
island, chiefly by noticing the absence of birds and
creatures familiar enough in many of my other
quarters, or the presence of some rarely met with
in rougher districts, but tempted to a summer
sojourn in this genial clime.

One of my last shooting quarters being in Mull,
a comparison of the two islands was a natural and

interesting subject of thought; for, although both
were situated on the west coast, and flanked by
mainland mountains which wooed the Atlantic
mists, there was yet a very perceptible difference
of climate, which the zoology of the islands quite
bears out.

To begin with the lowest order of animal life,
I was much surprised never to have encountered
one adder in Bute either last summer or this. In
Mull these reptiles perfectly swarm; and during
the dog-days I have counted half-a-dozen in the
course of a single forenoon. They seem to thrive
as well as multiply—many which I stumbled on
along the shores of Loch Baa being of immense
size. One of these monsters took possession of a
dry drain flanked by a stone dyke close to Glenforsa House. It had been attacked several times,
but always contrived to glide into the wall. If
the day was warm and sunny, there was the adder
on the bank; but it became so wary, after being
occasionally pelted with stones, that on hearing
the lightest step it slipped out of sight like magic.
I desired my people, by taking a circuit, not to
disturb it for a few days, and on a sultry morning

crouched noiselessly to the spot. The creature
was coiled up asleep, but the moment I raised
my stick it darted for the wall. I struck just as
its head entered the hole and stunned it. When
carrying it home alive by the tail, it disgorged a
full-grown field-mouse. On telling some neighbours what a capacious gorge this adder had, they
capped him with another killed on the opposite
coast of Morven the year before, of most prodigious length and girth, and in its belly was a full-
grown rat! As I could not at first swallow the rat
myself, I took the trouble to verify, as far as testi-
mony could verify, the gluttonous feat of this
python, and found I had been correctly informed.

A still more incredible story of a Mull adder I
give on my own authority. The reptile was basking close to a wall, when my son's tutor (now
minister of Kirkliston) threw a large stone, and
fairly halved it. The head and shoulders wriggled
into the wall, and he brought the tail to me.
Three days after he found the head half at the same
spot hale and hearty, and when attacked it hissed
and bit his stick fiercely. This adder was severed
about the centre, head and tail ends being of about

equal length. So prolific in adders was Mull that we have found them in winter coiled up in a heather bush, no doubt surprised and frozen to death by one of those pinching night frosts which often succeed the sunny butterfly-days of early winter.

The only serpent reptile I have detected in Bute is the familiar slow-worm. It is by no means plentiful here, although in Mull equally numerous with the adders. The rough ground of North Bute being well adapted to furnish food and shelter for reptiles, and the climate to foster them, why there are no adders and few blind-worms I do not pretend to guess.

The stoat abounds in Bute quite as much as in Mull, but the common weasel I have never seen but once.* A party of us surrounded and killed the creature last January, where it had taken refuge under a bush. It proved to be a beautiful example of the "cane" or "mousekiller," considered a distinct species by many English game-keepers. My own impression is that these mousekillers are only the young of the common

* Since writing the above I have twice detected full-grown specimens of the common weasel in Bute.

weasel, although some naturalists are inclined to
accord them the third class of our native weasels.
My tiny specimen is of course preserved as proof
that there are at least *canes* in Bute! Never
during the term of years I spent in Mull could I
detect a single instance of the common weasel;
and from inquiries I made in Skye, I am of
opinion that they are extinct there also.

The larger footed vermin, such as foxes, wild-
cats, martins, and (I think) foumarts, have most
likely never been introduced into this island, or,
if any of them were formerly indigenous, they
have been extirpated. Hedgehogs, however, are
far from rare, and my watcher trapped a brace of
them last spring at the same egg set for hoody-
crows. The first escaped, minus a foot, which
the man assured me had been the property of a
rat of such gigantic dimensions, that no cat in
Bute would be foolhardy enough to face him in
single combat. As if to solve the mystery, and
put a damper on his wonder and curiosity, next
night the other hedgehog was taken. These
prickly swine do great damage to all ground
nests of eggs within their sluggish beat.

None of the grander birds of prey breed in
Bute. The sea eagle sometimes rests for a day or
two when wandering south, or returning to her
mountains again from a winter migration. I
have, however, never seen a single instance of
the peregrine falcon, the hen harrier,* the golden
eagle, or the buzzard, all of which were far from
uncommon in Mull. Until lately ravens used
annually to hatch on the precipices of North
Bute, but for the last four years they have deserted their rocks. Still, on the evening of an
autumn or winter shooting-day, I am often warned by an iron croak from the clouds that the
corbie was scenting the carrion, and, followed by
her young ones, had swooped across the Kyles
from the shaggy mountains of Cowal, to feast
them in security on the island prey.

Of the accipitres, the only species I have verified in Bute are the sparrow-hawk and kestrel.
Once or twice I noticed in the distance what
might have been a female merlin; but as there

---

* Last autumn I perceived a female hen harrier or ringtail
skirting the shore of the Kyles, but it soon flew across to
Argyllshire.

have been no nests of that tiny falcon found on my heathery braes, the bird most likely was a male sparrow-hawk. Three of *their* nests were found by my watcher last spring, all fixed in stunted trees, the spontaneous growth of "dells without a name," in the midst of my best partridge breeding ground. We trapped the old male and female of two of these nests, and actually caught the third pair; but the female escaped by accidentally dropping a thrush she was feeding the young with between the jaws of the trap, which prevented them from holding, while the trap that caught the male unfortunately had a weak spring. After this warning, neither of course would return.

It is well understood by preservers of game that one hoody-crow, or even magpie, will destroy more grouse in the egg than a dozen eagles will do when they are fully fledged. On Kames and North Bute there were certainly far fewer black, but especially grey crows, than are generally met with on the west coast islands. We only discovered four nests this season, built as usual on the top boughs of tall trees, or on the stumps of bushes growing out of the face of a beetling cliff.

We trapped or poisoned the old couples of all the nests but one, placed far down in an inaccessible precipice. Two of these pairs were royston and carrion crows breeding together. In both cases the females were black, and the males grey. They had built in fir and oak trees, but the two couple which had nestled in the cliffs overhanging the sea were all grey roystons.

The number of magpies was so prodigious in North Bute that I often wondered how any lowland winged game had been raised at all.   With trap and poison we massacred eighteen couple of old birds, each pair having a nest full of eggs or young! Jesse, in his 'Gleanings,' mentions a knowing bird-dealer, who affirmed that there were two species of magpie. The smaller kind, which he termed "the bush magpie," always built in bushes or hedgerows, while the larger ones chose the tops of high slender trees. By far the greater proportion of those destroyed by me last spring had their nests in low scrubby bushes among the thick cover of North Bute. The Kames magpies, however, all built on the tops of high larches or firs. There was no perceptible difference in size of the old birds of the two districts ; and it appeared evident that the reason why those at Kames were so aspiring in the situation of their high-roofed nurseries, was the absence of cover to conceal them ; and by far the greater proportion of these sly birds put more trust in their own well-known hidling powers among the thickets of North Bute, than in the pinnacle of the most tall and dizzy fortress that nature ever reared.

It is now thirty-seven years since the secret of trapping flying vermin, by removing their young from the nest and using them as decoys, was first found out by myself and my late father's gamekeeper. The day of our discovery rises clearly to my mind's eye from beyond the deepening mists of these long years; and somewhat gloomily too, for on that very day I was the means of expelling from the loch of my ancestors the most romantic and time-honoured dependant on its bounty.

Having arranged a vermin crusade with the keeper among the islands of Loch Lomond, the ospreys, who had just repaired their yearly nest on the ivied castle of Galbreath, were unfortunately too tempting sport for a thoughtless youth and a destructive gamekeeper. My first exploit, after being concealed on the islet, was to shoot the female, while my ally, selecting the trustiest of his " stamps," fixed a sea-trout found in the eyrie on the plate, and set the trap. We then rowed to the adjacent twin islands, forming " the straights " of Loch Lomond, where no less than four couple of vindictive carrion crows had each a nest of " hopefuls," within a few days of beginning their apprenticeship to the nefarious trade of the family. It was of no use to watch four nests for the chance of shooting the old crows, but a smart thought struck us—Why should we not use the young as *bait* in the circle of twigs? Immediately the four nests were emptied into twig-circles at the foot of their respective trees, and the traps set.

On our return the same evening, the poor osprey widower was fast in his trap, and next morning the female " hoody " of all four nests was in the same predicament. The traps were reset, and the " he-ones" of two of the nests taken; but the other pair of males had been so scared at the plight of their struggling mates, as to allow the young to perish rather than venture to feed

them. To obviate this, I have lately adopted the
plan of setting two circles of twigs, *out of sight of
each other*, and putting half the young in one
circle and half in the other. Should an old bird
be trapped, I change the young to a fresh circle
of boughs a little way off. The surviving old bird
will readily come to the fresh-set circle, although
nothing would induce it to risk itself where it
saw its helpmate so mysteriously in grief. I have
in contemplation a trap for winged vermin which
will quite supersede the iron one and circle of
twigs. If my plan matures, from its open appearance, the most shy birds will venture on this
trap; and when they do, escape is impossible.

The familiar kestrel is equally well distributed
in Bute as on the mainland. Distinct in manners
and habits from both the falcons and hawks, this
bird is no less perfectly endowed for the part
assigned to it by Nature's law. Anchored in the
air by that power of wing peculiar to this *day owl,*
it plies the trade of mouse-hunting alike on the
heathery hill or the cultivated field. Mice being
most rife in the dusk, the kestrel is the latest
hunter of the hawks, and is of course gifted with

a larger eye to collect the last rays of failing light. Although they have no objection to birds, *when they can catch them*, and prowl *all day* to provide for their nestlings, I consider kestrels less hurtful to game than the ivy owl which flies entirely *by night*, and my opinion is borne out by the feeding hoards of both when they have young. It is a fact that kestrels have far less difficulty in providing their nestlings with a constant supply of field-mice than the brown owl has; and this is accounted for by the kestrel's power of wing, which enables her to keep the air with the same ease as those buoyant owls which live exclusively on mice. The last summer I fished Loch Baa a pair of these birds were rearing their young close to "the Salmon Point." Every time I fished the point the hawks flew round screaming, while I assured my oarsman (a poacher from Salen) that they did no harm to game, and much good to the farmer. The man could scarcely conceal a sneer, until one afternoon the screamer dashed out of the wood, within a few yards of our heads, with a large field-mouse dangling in its claws. "I see'd its tail an' legs as plain as the boat," he repeated again and again.

I knew of four kestrels' nests on my Bute
shootings last spring, most picturesquely placed
on lonely points of rock, but did not permit any
of them to be molested, with the exception of
a young one, which my boys reared along with
a sparrow-hawk of the same age. They never
quarrelled, got into fine feather about the end
of July, and seemed quite contented in their
enormous cage. The kestrel once escaped, and
flew about the old trees and tower in a restless
unhappy manner, and seemed delighted when it
found the way back to captivity, not unlike those
inhabitants of the city suburb, who have learned
to prefer their close den to the wildest freedom.

I am sorry to bring a case of poaching against
the respectable and industrious rook ; but in dry
seasons, when the parched ground refuses the
usual supply of slugs and worms, these birds are
very destructive among the eggs of the pheasant
or partridge preserve. The charge of devouring
young birds has never, so far as my research goes,
been brought home to rooks, although members
of the same order, but partners in a smaller firm,
have been convicted of kidnapping and murder-

ing pheasants a few days old. Two pairs of jack-
daws, after a long drought, were shot in the act
of picking up pheasants from the coops as soon
as they were hatched, to satisfy the craving of
their voracious families. I am convinced, however, that these evil deeds are exceptional, and
that almost any bird, as well as omnivorous crows,
when deprived of its favourite food, can subsist
and even thrive on what it likes far less, and
would indeed otherwise reject.

An appropriate rookery surrounds the old castle
here, and to watch the order and discretion of the
sable colony when superintending the education
of their respective families was a favourite pas-
time of mine all last spring. From the time they
emerge from the wicker nursery, and are promoted to the schoolroom as " branchers," the
system of rook instruction begins. They are
taught to use a convenient bough always above
the nest, and the parents, in bringing food, approach the nest-tree where they can be first dis-
cerned from this look-out twig. At first, when
fed, the perchers were apt to plump down into
the nest ; but soon becoming stronger, they hopped

and fluttered from spray to spray, but always
above the sheltering nest, and ready to drop into
it at the warning caw of the old ones. The flapping wings and eager calls of the young often
warned me that the parents were approaching
long before I saw them myself, and I was often
amazed at the *intuition* of the different young
broods in detecting the approach of their own
father or mother among the black multitude
hovering and cawing in the air. The branchers
were not encouraged to take an adventurous flight
to the adjacent tree until quite strong and fully
fledged ; after this they soon learned to follow the
flock to the adjoining feeding grounds.

From their cheerful social habits inviting observation and study, rooks and the interior eco-
nomy of their commonwealth have furnished
matter for many curious tales. I give the following instance, which only took place in the year
1863 : There had been for years a rook's nest on
a tree in the back garden of a house in Moray
Place. During the winter of 1863 a large company of rooks pulled it quite down. The following spring a pair rebuilt the nest, laid eggs, and

began to sit. An immense troop of their black
kindred soon surrounded them, killed the male,
who fell into the area, slew the female on her
eggs, tore off one of her wings, and all the pirates
disappeared as suddenly as they came, and never
revisited the place—except, indeed, one solitary
spy, which flew round and round the house the
morning after the massacre, making a great noise.
The butler picked up the slain rook and the female's wing, while the family watched with wonder
the storming of the nest and the double murder.

A gentleman living in Newbattle Terrace, at
the south side of Edinburgh, told me a curious
rook anecdote that happened last spring. Being
unwilling to allow a colony from a neighbouring
rook settlement to take possession of the old trees
around his house, he shot the female of the first
couple that built a nest on them. The widower
paired again directly, and brought the new mate
to the same house, when she shared the fate of the
first. The determined settler immediately took to
himself a third partner, and installed her into
the fatal lodging. After her death the rooks
assembled in a body, and tore down the nest.

My authority for these facts is unimpeachable, and at the service of any one who thinks it worth while to demand it.

It may be from their uniform black inviting attention, but no birds show the Albino stain more frequently than blackbirds or rooks. I have seen these opposite "extremes" of colour "meet" in the rook almost every season. I shot a young one in the rookery here with a white bill, another with white nails to its toes; a third had white wings, the most common phase of this *lusus naturæ*. The contradiction of a whole nest of white blackbirds, and another of white rooks, in both cases the parents being black, was the most unaccountable freak that nature could possibly play.*

* A notice of a white sparrow in the ' Scotsman' gave rise to this reply :—

"WHITE SPARROWS.

"KAMES CASTLE, *Oct.* 10, 1865.

"SIR,—The white sparrow of Leith Walk is not the *rara avis* the correspondents of the ' Scotsman ' suppose.

"I have one in my collection at 1 Royal Terrace, shot by my son in the barrack square of Dundalk. In the same case is another with white wings, shot by myself at a farm-steading near Joppa. Another buff sparrow haunts the village of Port-Bannatyne, close to this place. Another white-winged

H

When the month of December is mild, rooks build, thrushes sing, blackcocks croon, wood-pigeons coo, martin swallows sometimes appear, and even butterflies have been known to show themselves. Editors of newspapers are often bored at Christmas with accounts of some one or other of these wonders, which so often occur every mild winter season.

Another interesting section of the omnivora, the starlings, are very numerous here. They come in clouds every evening to roost on the old beeches and elms, close to and even among the rooks. Hidling in their nesting habits, they cannot be watched so easily as rooks ; but by the common mode of fixing boxes to the higher branches of a tall tree, we induced two pairs to adopt a ready-made home. I liked better, however, to see them choose their own site among the thick ivy of the garden wall, where several pairs hatch every year. Of course my boys tamed one this summer, which

sparrow I see almost every day when going to shoot in the north end of the island. The Port-Bannatyne bird I saw all last season as well as this.—I am, &c.

"JOHN COLQUHOUN."

has proved the most pleasant and amusing of pets. It was early taught to quit its cage in the kitchen and devour the flies, which were so dexterously snapped up that one's eye often could not follow the capture. The windows are never shut when "the stare" is hunting, and it often flies round the lawn for half-a-day, but always comes back to its cage before dusk. Our starling, however, is not sentimental, and, if he were, has no right to the plaintive plea, " I can't get out."

One feels a kind of reverence for those birds whose life is spent in the silence and solemnity of night; and the music in which they vent their contemplations, though always in the minor key, is listened to with more interest, and perhaps scarcely less pleasure, than that of sunshine and the day. The spectre-like ways and melancholy hootings of these night-lovers please well the fancy; while the oft-repeated plaint of the wood-owl, from ivied tree or mouldering tower, is answered, perhaps, by some inner second of our own. Even the wild screech of the white owl, as it flits stealthily and rapidly along, has a power over us peculiarly its own ; and one is amazed that so true

a poet as Cowper could class the call of these honoured sages "even beneath the harsh tones of the
jay, the pye, the daw." Surely he could never
have listened to them under the canopy of heaven,
but only caught the sound from his own drawing-
room, with all the curtains closed.

The country around this venerable castle seems
especially adapted to rear both white and brown
owls. A mixture of cultivated and waste land,
interspersed with woody dells, old ruins, and hollow trees, ought to have attracted them from the
mainland opposite coast, where they always breed;
yet, though constantly watching, I have never seen
or heard either of the more common species,*
while the rarest (the short-eared owl) twice unexpectedly presented herself on Kames Hill when
I was ranging for grouse.

About the beginning of August 1864, I was
examining the ground with a view to the 12th,
and my dogs "poked up" this owl, when she flew
a little distance and pitched on the top of a bing

---

* Some time after the above was penned, a white or barn
owl took possession of the garden-wall ivy—the only one I
have seen in Bute.

of stones capping a heathery mound. My youngest
son, a schoolboy, was my only companion, and of
course wished me to go home for a gun while he
watched the owl. Not having a specimen in my
collection, I was much tempted, but finally decided that, as the bird would most likely haunt the
place, we would always give the owl's cairn a trial
when grouse-shooting near it. All the early part
of last season I never passed the mound without
a close look-out; but the searches became more
careless each succeeding time, and at last were
omitted altogether. On the morning of the 4th of
September of the present year, thirteen months
after we first saw this rare bird, I was after grouse
with *the same companion,* close to "the hoolet's
cairn," as he called it, when of her own accord she
rose at some distance from us, and I shot her. It
was but seldom that my youngest boy was with
me on my shooting excursions ; and, considering
my many trials for *the* owl with one or other of
his brothers, that he should have been the only
one out the day she fell might have furnished good
material for a superstitious Highland legend.

The far more common long-eared owl I have

never seen hunting here, but once or twice last winter I distinctly heard its scream close to the castle windows, and a few months since my gillie lad brought me a half-grown one, found in a dying state on the lawn. It seemed starved to death, being a perfect skeleton.

I have listened both last summer and this for the drowsy chur of another favourite bird of the dusk, the fearless night-jar. That this migrant should prefer Mull to Bute, where night-moths are so plentiful, seems to me unreasonable. Not one fern owl have I seen or heard on the northern district of this island, while in Mull the monotonous spinning-wheel note was raised each July evening close to both our shooting quarters; and I have preserved the finest male specimen I ever saw, which I shot one 12th of August, raised from the heather by my dogs.

The more obtrusive and noticeable day migrants, such as the cuckoo, the landrail, and the swallow tribe, seem to revel in our neighbourhood, while fly-catchers and white-throats delight the eye with their graceful movements among the laurel bushes. From entries in my journal, I find that, on the 5th of May, when we returned to our island home, "Cuckoos and landrails are in full cry, and chimney swallows are flying in considerable numbers. Neither the window martin nor swift has yet appeared. The gardener told me that he first saw a swallow and heard the cuckoo on the same day, the 30th of April." " Monday, 22d May.*—Window martins begun to build in the eaves of the old tower. Saw, on the 18th, the first and only pair of swifts I have noticed here this season. Heard yesterday morning, at twenty-five minutes past three A.M., two cuckoos, two landrails, a thrush, a sedge-warbler, and other birds, all singing and calling at the same moment. The landrail in the clover field, and the sedge-warbler among the laurels, never cease their love-call during the darkest night." " Friday, June 9th.—The pair of swifts attempting to take possession of the same martin's nest they stormed last year."

* A daughter of the late Lord President Hope gave me the following curious and interesting particulars of a swallow's nest which she had often heard told by her eminent father :— A pair had built their nest in a corner of the Lord President's window. The fabric, however, always fell, until two older swallows *built it for them,* and then left them in possession.

This season the bold attack of the swifts was finally repulsed by the determined resistance of the martins. From coming early last year, the black pirates had little difficulty in seizing the newly-made home of the industrious builders; but this time the martins fought with desperation in defence of their young as well as home, so the pair of swifts, after their defeat, took easy possession of an empty martin's nest at Kames Villa, where my neighbour tells me they are bringing up a thriving family. I marked the incubation and daily feeding of the young swifts last year until they took wing; I then carefully watched them each day till they left us for the arid plains of Africa. My last entries were Monday the 1st of August, Tuesday the 2d, and Wednesday the 3d, after which date I saw none in Bute till my note of them last May.

All birds feeding in the air live on winged insects, and all feeders on winged insects must be migrants. No better type of both visits this country than the bird last mentioned. It is the fleetest and strongest-winged of all British birds. For ten long hours of a July day, without resting, will

this indefatigable creature dart through the air at
an immense height, collecting the higher-flying insects with its flat-shaped beak, the gape of which, as
in all the swallows, is admirably adapted for hoard-
ing the treasure. I once counted about a dozen
black flies in the gape of some newly-shot swifts.
So exclusively is this large swallow a bird of the
air, that it never alights except when scrambling
into its nest, and if placed on flat ground, from
the weakness of its feet and length of its wings,
would be unable to rise. The feet, exactly like a
small hand, are totally unfitted for walking, and
only serve the purpose of clutching the eaves of a
house when seeking the nesting-place. Feeding
higher in the air than the other swallows, their
insect-food fails soonest, so they come later and
leave earlier than any of the other swallows.
Three months is their usual time with us, while
the other three species of swallow—viz., the chimney one and the window and bank martins—not
only come earlier, but stay two months later.
I saw a bank martin in the south of England on
the 25th of last November, and on the 5th of
December following another pair hawking for

insects among the house-tops of Henley-on-Thames. I never before remember seeing these birds so late in departure.

The range of the chimney swallow and the two martins comes much nearer the ground than that of the swift. They often alight, and, from the conformation of their feet and shorter wings, can easily rise again. The weaker wing is made up for by the stronger foot, which gives these swallows the power of resting on house-tops, rails, or even on the ground itself.

Full before my window a pair of fly-catchers keep continually darting from the rails of a wooden bridge after insects on the wing. These birds may be called the next in succession to swallows, for although they live much on the ground they find the chief of their food in the air. They arrive here a little later than the swallows, and depart shortly before them.

On the broad planks of the bridge grey and yellow wagtails find a constant supply. These graceful creatures, although occasionally catching a fly in the air, keep almost constantly on the ground, where their active feet and legs enable them to chase their prey with great activity. Emphatically a ground bird, the wagtail is not confined to winged insects, but feeds much on worms and the eggs of land and water flies. This subsistence does not cease entirely in winter; hence it does not migrate, or only partially so, from colder to milder places in our own country.

The rich fields of Bute team with skylarks. These general favourites feed in summer on the field insects and earthworms, in winter almost entirely on the seeds of annual weeds scattered over the corn stubbles. Totally independent of trees, they are the free songsters of the air, and from fields without a hedge, or upland slopes without a bush, trill forth their melody so charming to our ear, while the figure of the little syren, twittering in a flood of light, is wholly lost to our ken.

The larks introduce the buntines, the first of the hard-billed birds. Some of them approach the larks in their habits, by living much in cultivated fields, and refusing to perch on trees. They all have bills formed for breaking the rinds of seeds. They also eat insects moderately. I have

never seen the common buntine in Bute, nor the
snow species all last winter.   I have an Albino of
the former in my collection, shot by my son at
Fort-George.

Immense flocks of finches congregate here all
winter, and are most useful to the farmer, consum-
ing the seeds of troublesome weeds which otherwise would overrun the country.   Where the land
is poorer the finches migrate southward in winter,
returning again to the north, when they separate
to breed.

Green finches, and, of course, chaffinches, build
near this old castle—the goldfinch and greyfinch
among the whins of the neighbouring brakes.
Although so hard - billed, all these finches eat
caterpillars and other insects moderately.   The
truest seed-eater of the race is the goldfinch ; its
favourite food being thistle, chickweed, and dan-
delion seeds.   The green and grey finches are
very partial to flax and lint seeds—hence their
name of green and grey linties or linnets.

In describing the birds around this ivied tower
of Bute, any one with a turn for natural history
will at once perceive that I have, link by link,

connected the most perfect of the soft - billed
migrants of the air (the swift) with the hardest-
billed resident (the goldfinch) which collects food
on the ground. Like all God's works, there are
no gaps in ornithology—one species glides into
another until they are dovetailed into one har-
monious whole.

In crossing the Minch some years since, a little
dark bird was constantly flitting past our cutter
with all the characteristics of a swallow—powerful wings, long tail, body thrown well forward,
and tapering like a canoe. Seamen have a superstitious dread that this sea-swallow brings storms,
and delights in them. But the truth is, that
"stormy petrels" dislike the tempest as much as
their neighbours, as it is only when the sea is
tolerably quiet that they can collect the chief
part of their food, which consists of the oily sub-
stance on the top of the waters. When the waves
rise, of course the surface of the sea is much increased, which disperses the oil, and gives far
more trouble in collecting it ; add to which, the
birds are so light and buoyant, partly from their
greasy food, that, like the thistle - down, they ap-

pear the sport of the hurricane. When feeding they use both wings and feet, and while the former are expanded the latter tip the water, so the little bird appears both flying and walking. It is on account of this kind of "walking on the water" they derive their name of Petrels or little Peters.

It was a lovely June night when I crossed the Minch, and many a sea-swallow was skimming in two senses ocean's calm bosom. When they were preening off the collected oil its effect made the bird so light that, like a gossamer, it seemed to touch the sea, but not to press it.

In size, shape, rapidity of flight, as well as endurance on wing, sweeping even over the broad Atlantic, petrels bear a close resemblance to the common chimney swallow. But if the joyous sunny swallow, always associated with verdure and beauty, has this ocean delegate equally suggestive of clouds and tempest, it has also a representative among the sombre birds of night. The night-jar, familiarly known as the "night-hawk," not only connects the owls with insect-feeders, but also forms the link between swallows and owls. Like the swallow tribe, it is a migrant and insect-feeder ; preying on the night-moths, beetles, and cockchafers, by following and capturing them in the air as swallows seize day insects. Indeed, the capricious evolutions of this twilight spectre bear close resemblance to the sportive wheels of the bird of summer sunshine. It has been called "the night-swallow," just as stormy petrels are commonly known to sailors as swallows of the ocean.

From hiding in the day-time in brakes of fern, the night-jar is also appropriately styled "the fern owl ;" and indeed the silky feathers, noiseless flight, large eye, dusky colour, and nocturnal life of this bird, quite entitle it to a low niche among the owls ; while the insect-food, migratory habits, large gape, soft beak, and weak feet, prove it equally akin to the swallow family, which right I have just claimed. The night-swallow has the advantage over the day one in a hair-netting on each side of the bill—a very great assistance in night-hunting, but not needed and therefore not given to the bird of the sunlight.

To a heedless listener, the song or call of each

individual of any particular species of bird may appear exactly alike, but there is often consider- able variety. Song-bird fanciers know this well ; but in their case it may be urged that domestica- tion and care have altered and drawn out the voices of their favourites, just as judicious farmers improve their stock. But I take as illustrations the most obtrusive and monotonous of our day and night birds, and to a fine ear scarcely any two of them will be found in the same key. There are also prominent and exceptional points of difference in the call of a particular cuckoo, as well as in the hoot of an eccentric ivy owl.

A cuckoo that haunted our garden all last spring and summer, and was most useful in grub- bing up the cabbage and gooseberry caterpillars, put an additional note into its pipe. When a neighbour cuckoo from the near hill, and another from the beeches on the lawn, struck up the rub- rical coo-coo, they were always replied to by the innovator's coo-coo-coo. We made him a D.D., and the "Dr" had perhaps as much reason for the change in his ritual as if his degree had come from the Senatus of Edinburgh itself. When fishing

St Mary's Loch with a friend, the cracked voice of one cuckoo contrasted oddly with half-a-dozen others scattered through the neighbouring woods. We were lashing opposite sides of the loch, and the first question asked on meeting was—" Did you hear the cracked cuckoo ?"

Although living close to the old trees where the brown owls hoot every night, some people are so unobservant as never to have remarked that the " dismal bird" has two calls. The first is one prolonged note, followed a few seconds after by a juggling imitation. The owl then rests its voice a longer or shorter time according to its whim, without any approach to regularity in these intervals. But not to hear the second trembling hoot of a brown owl immediately following the first clear note, is rare indeed ; and I have only remarked this in the case of one or two innovating owls among the many I have listened to under the spring or autumnal moonshine.

There are no rock-doves in Bute, but great numbers of ring-doves (the common wood-pigeon) fully supply their place. All spring the groves are soothed with the love-note of this ornamental

I

bird ; and when searching for vermin last May, the
constant crash of the wood-dove from her wicker
saucer of two eggs, gave token of flocks that would
congregate in autumn and never separate until
"the time of the singing of birds is come, and the
voice of the turtle is heard in the land."

When the fruits and berries of early harvest
begin to ripen, numberless small companies of
wood-pigeons shelter in the shaggy copses of the
Kyles, which soon unite into large assemblies
under the spreading branches of the old beech-
trees, to regale on their delicious nuts. So long
as there is abundance of this beech-mast food our
lawn beeches attract their myriads, which vie with
the rooks and starlings in giving cheerfulness and
animation even among the sere and yellow leaves
of the shortening day.

The fine shoals of white fish that used to haunt
the bays of Bute, have of late years considerably
deserted them. In winter multitudes of " herring
hakes" are captured with the net—many of large
size. I saw hampers full on Port-Bannatyne quay
all last January. They are good food when cut
into steaks and fried. A few days ago, a boy

brought me a basket of five very broad-shaped fish
with red fins, like the bream or "braise" of Loch
Lomond. They were more than a pound in weight,
and he only asked a penny for each, and was
quite pleased with sixpence for the lot. He called
them "silver haddies," but I rather think "sea
perch" is the proper name. He caught them with
a hand-line, and a bit of herring for bait. During
a whole season I fished Loch Long very successfully, both with herring and mussel bait, and with
hand and long lines, but I never either caught or
heard of this "silver haddy" in that branch sea-
loch of the Firth of Clyde.

When driving along the Kyles for a day's par-
tridge-shooting on one of the northern farms of
Bute, a whale of about 30 feet long rose close to
the shore. On overtaking the gillie, whom we
had sent forward with the evening relay of dogs,
he assured us with a face of awe that the whale
had become dangerous in the night, and driven the
fishermen ashore. Had it been one of the Arctic
whales, not unfrequent in the Sound of Mull, the
angry freak of the leviathan would have been characteristic enough; but as the present monster of

the deep was only a bottle-nose, or "black-fish," it was evident that the boatmen had made the lad swallow a story "very like the fierce fish," whose startling *entrée* had whetted his appetite for the terrible.

On questioning the fishers next day, they laughed heartily, saying it was true that a black-fish had broken a net some miles below, and that the one we saw had begun to blow and lash the water with its tail, but these vagaries were only signs of anxiety lest its young one, which no doubt was near, might get among the boats and nets. In place of dreading these small whales, the fishers were always glad of their company, as harbingers of a successful night's fishing; and about the same time last year I watched an old female bottle-nose and two young ones gambolling among the fleet of "scows," while the crews looked kindly at them as the jackals of their trade.

Prodigious droves of porpoises also hang upon the herring shoals. The smaller kind, called "pelluchs," often spring several yards out of the water, and come down with a thump that may be heard in calm weather more than a mile off, while the white foam caused by their fall in the sea can be distinguished at double that distance. Frequently, in my walks or shooting excursions along the shores of the island, I see more than a hundred of these creatures rolling, splashing, or springing clear of the sea like fresh-run salmon.

A solitary grey seal has for some years frequented the rocks above Ettrick Bay. The old hermit shows himself when the bag-nets proclaim the annual influx of salmon to the bay, and cruises about the coast so long as the fish remain. Last year " the grey sealch " was seldom out of the shallow water, and my watcher was always reminding me to bring my rifle barrels—especially when the weather was warm and calm. One day, when shooting on Glenmore and Ettrick side, he would fain have changed my gun into a rifle, for the seal had been so bold that morning as to prevent his wife from filling her pitcher at the spring. " The beast," quoth she, pathetically, " pat up its awfu' coorse head close to me an' the bairns—I was feerd it wad come ashore an' tak' ane o' them awa."

Once or twice I walked down to the bay armed and ready, but the enemy was either invisible, or plying his piratical vocation among the salmon far beyond reach of my bullets. This year he has not put in an appearance at all; and a few years since he also absented himself for a whole salmon season, but returned on the following one at the usual time. The many years that the Ettrick seal has summered in its bay has gained for it some local notoriety, while its curious and methodical habits have so far interested me as to stop all desire to put an end to its wild and wayward life.

Not being an entomologist, my observation of the insects of Bute has been very circumscribed. I have seen none of the southern butterflies or moths which the mild climate of this island had led me to expect. Neither cockchafers nor stag-beetles enliven the twilight, and not one specimen of the larger sphynxes have we captured, or even seen. Had there been any, no doubt some of these gorgeously-pencilled beauties would have found their way into our drawing-room, along with the sober-coloured small moths which beset our gas-lustres every warm, dark night, as both sides of our glass door into the garden were left open, when the gas was lit, and long after darkness set in.

In the summer of 1864, wasps' nests were not only more numerous than I ever saw them anywhere else, but their size was also enormous. There were at least a dozen close to the castle and garden. I have long had in my little museum what I considered as fine a specimen of the wasps' hive as it was possible to procure; but two of these from Bute (one built in a hedge adjoining the garden, the other fixed to a currant bush in the very midst of the fruit) were nearly double the circumference of my preserved paragon. This year, although the fruit has been fully as plentiful, and the season equally fine, there have been scarcely any wasps' nests, and the few we have discovered are wretched weedy productions, scarcely deserving the name.

As if in contrast to the wasps of the present year, the wild bees have thriven amazingly. My boys found no less than nine "binks" along the banks of the brooklet that feeds the duck pond.

These hives comprised the yellow "foggy" bee, the small and large humble bee, and one hive of red-hipped bees. In the evening we often removed the thatching, and inspected the grubs and honeycomb of the foggy bees' hives. Some were much more cross and dangerous when disturbed than their neighbours; and it is a rule acted on by schoolboys, that when wild bees hive under ground, and they fail to reach them the first digging, it is useless to attempt a second, for the swarm will remove or destroy the honey on the first alarm from the spade.

It is a curious fact that honey bees don't like the flowers or heather of Tighnabruach. They therefore fly across the Kyles to Bute and gather honey there. In returning laden, however, they are unable to recross the sea, and multitudes are found drowned. There is no honey to be had in Tighnabruach in consequence. They thrive well in Bute, for, last summer, my boys took a hive in the old tower of Kames Castle full of splendid honey.

Had more southern night-insects found their way to the genial climate of Bute, they might

probably have been followed by the great bat—
Vespertilio altivolans of naturalists. This night-
flyer takes the same place among bats that swifts
do among swallows. Like swifts, their flight is
rapid and high, and the term of their appearance
equally short. I have watched them from Henley
Bridge coursing over the Thames among the other
bats, which looked, in comparison, no bigger than
butterflies. They shelter during the day in hollow
trees, but never under the slates or leads of houses
or out-buildings, the favourite refuge of the two
other species of British bat. I have one of the
Henley great bats stuffed, and, barring its colour
(a rich chestnut), it is precisely like a giant of the
smaller common kind.

The top of the old tower here is a city of bats.
On raising the lead sheeting about the beginning
of last summer, we discovered hundreds both of
long-eared and little bats, each female having her
piccaninny attached by its tiny claws to her breast.
When hunting in the twilight, they carry their
young one too ; and the little creature is so deftly
and firmly fastened as not in the least to incom-
mode the parent, or hinder her success in moth-

hunting. The mothers nurse their young ones in
this way, which are the most horrid imps it is
possible to fancy.

The grousing of this island would never suit
many of the sportsmen-migrants who crowd our
moors in August and September. The *battue*
system from the south has been so successfully
applied, even to Scotch moors, that in all our
first-class ranges the difference between good and
bad sportsmen or good and bad dogs is scarcely
noticeable. If the man is a fair shot, little else
will be required of him; while his dogs, if
superior ones, are wasted on such ground, and
may even have their mettle slacked, their hunting powers weakened, and their instinct dwarfed,
from finding multitudes of birds without working
for them. To my mind, sixty or eighty brace
killed on these swarming beats deserves to be
placed in the same category as a pheasant drive,
or shooting rabbits in a teeming warren.

The moors which give most pleasure and satisfaction to a true and able sportsman are those
which, with the aid of first-rate dogs, will afford
a bag of from twenty to thirty-five brace. On

such ground he can watch with delight the instinct which his high-couraged and keen-scented
dogs throw into their work ; his own knowledge
of the sport and walking powers will have full
scope ; and should his bag be up to the mark at
the end of the day, he can feel satisfied that it
was scientifically and pluckily filled.

In the above remarks I only allude to men
who lay claim to be called the *élite* of the shooting world. A predecessor of mine, in a grouse
tenancy, candidly told me that he gave up the
moor, as he had to wander so long without a
shot that he was likely to miss from nervous-
ness. I also suspected that his kennel was none
of the best, for during the term of his lease he
never exceeded four brace of grouse in one day ;
while the first 12th I shot over the hill, with
first-rate dogs, my bag was nineteen brace, and
from ten to fifteen during August and the first
weeks of September. This gentleman immediately took a moor in Perthshire, and the first
day bagged fifty brace. I cordially wished him
joy, and felt convinced that a prolific moor was
the place for a nervous shot with indifferent dogs.

Few will deny that the man who habitually brings home the heaviest game-bag has every claim to be called, if not the best shot, certainly the most accomplished sportsman of his party. To apply the test fairly, however, we must exclude those teeming high-priced moors where good shooting *alone* is required, and stick to those second-rate beats where birds must be searched for with patient skill, and shot down with dexterity and *unfailing nerve*. The shooter who generally makes "the score" on such ground would only rarely find his shooting match with a fowling-piece all over the world.

The seasons 1864-5 (the two first of my lease of Kames and North Bute) were good breeding years, and the birds free of disease on most of the Scotch moors. By the 12th of the present year they were very strong on wing, and from unsettled broken weather much wilder than usual. My team of sporting dogs is, however, most efficient, and consists of a brace of very superior Irish setters, an old English pointer bitch, admirable for close hunting, and a dropper (the cross of a celebrated Russian pointer dog with an ex-

cellent smooth bitch) which can work all day
and never cry "enough." The whole four are
hard workers, have exquisite noses, never get
footsore, and are perfectly steady on all game.
My retriever "Auk" completes the lot, and in
my whole sporting experience I have only had
one to equal, none to surpass him.

Bad weather at the 12th does not annoy me, as
I have no objection to allow a week or ten days'
" cheeper law." This year I did not shoot till the
22d, and had the comfort of never hearing a
squeak all day. The morning was dull, and
heavy mists lowered on the peaks of Arran and
the Argyllshire mountains. In face of this the
barometer steadily rose, and being seconded by a
few breaks of the clouds, it was decided to send
forward the mid-day relief of dogs, with orders
to return should the weather fail.

Scarcely had we left the lodge gate when a de-
pressing drop of rain fixed all eyes on the horizon.
A fine bit of blue, large enough even for a Hol-
lander's tarpaulins, decided the point in favour of
the day; but the " spitty " rain did not cease for
some time, and was sufficiently damping to turn

homeward the gillie and his dogs. He joyously faced about again, assuring us he would be at the farmhouse where we meant to put up our car almost as soon as we should. It was now about nine, and the lad's directions were to meet us on the hill with the provision-basket and fresh dogs at two o'clock.

At a quarter to ten I uncoupled on the crest of Clochnabae. The heather was at first so wet as to preclude immediate hope of close shots; but the sun was blinking out, and would soon make it dry enough. On circling round the hill, first one good pack, then another, each led by the jeering crow of the old cock, rose merrily in the very line of our range. At this moment a large red hare sprang at my feet; and although unwilling to encumber my game-carrier with such lumber, I rolled her over in very spite. First blood of season 1865; but then it was only footed, not winged gore. Sun out now, and heath drying fast. Still another pack rose wild, and dogs beginning to look unhappy. Turned into the sunny side of the hill, where the raised packs had preceded me. Dogs ranging, free and true, but my first flying as well as running shot was fired without their aid. A fine pack rose at my feet, and I killed one, knocking feathers out of another with my second barrel—one of the few escapes of the day. First bird in the bag at half-past eleven.

The red Irishman now settled to a point, beautifully backed by the Saxon bitch. A fine chance, and slew my brace. The next pack, found by old Juno, rose sharp, but I got my couple of birds again. The canine, working with spirit and supporting each other well, made no mistakes; and although much of the game rose provokingly wild, they procured me some excellent chances, and we met the gillie and relay of dogs with nine brace of fine full-grown birds.

The Glenmore valley cuts right through the further hills of Bute. Hitherto I had kept to the north end, having parcelled out the southern division for the evening sport. Before crossing to the fresh range, I gave the ridge and sheltered face of the hunted hill a trial with the fresh dogs for broken birds. If a beat for scattered game has been judiciously chosen, and the shooter humours it by a series of circles and *detours,* with the aid of trustworthy dogs, the bag rapidly and pleasantly fills.

When a young and impatient grouse-shooter, I had a useful lesson on scattered birds, which has often since encouraged me to perseverance and helped me to success. On that day, many years ago, I had reserved my best dogs for the evening, and after some successful morning shooting on the hill-top had broken and scattered some fine packs. Most of the birds had topped the ridge slanting downwards, and I felt certain of heavy shooting whenever I had sufficiently worked the higher peaks. The steep ground and warm sun had been severe, and when I began to hunt for the scattered game, my dogs showed signs of having done their work. Still they fought bravely on, but, with the exception of a solitary cock, did not stumble on any of the birds we had driven down. Feeling sure that we had passed through the midst of them, I proposed to take a second stretch along the brow with the evening dogs, even in the face of my watcher's protest that we should lose two valuable hours seeking for game that "wasna there." Scarcely were the fresh dogs free than they found grouse. Another and another point in quick succession, while the game, in threes, pairs, or single birds, rose at my feet. In place of two lost hours they were equal to any four of the rest of the day for regular and deadly chances. It was only the same over again in Bute, and my brow range of Clochnabae hill added three brace to the bag.

An old gamekeeper used to say at starting, " I'll try for so many brace, but dinna expec' aboon the half o't." I had set my bag at twenty brace, but did not " expec' aboon" fifteen. It was past four when we crossed the valley of Glenmore, and scaled the evening hill, so to make eight brace on Bute moors in the few hours now at our service would tolerate few misses. Even of this short time more than an hour elapsed before we got among the packs ; but when we did, the dropper behaved splendidly. Finding at long distance, and never making a false point, she gave us every opportunity to break the game on the very heights we had selected. The scent had been good all day, and at length the birds began to sit pretty well too. They were found by the

K

dogs in their best style, while I seconded them by shooting at the top of my bent ; and at a quarter to eight the gillie threw up his glengarry with a hurrah for the twenty brace.

My next grousing day, on the 26th, was devoted to the nearer moors of Kames. A high east wind spoilt the scent, and made the game still more fretty and shy of a point than on the 22d. My journal entry says—"Killed eleven brace ; only let off one shot, and three badly-hit birds." On the 30th, was assisted by my eldest son, who had got a few days' leave from his regiment. Our united bag was twenty-one and a half brace, four hares, and a snipe. My journal again records— "Both of us shot in our best style, and dogs did their part equally well." Wednesday, September 6th, took a rambling stretch with my son over the greater part of our grouse ground for his con- cluding day. At eleven o'clock heavy rain came on, and stopped our sport till near one ; but the clouds then parted, a hot sun dried the heath, and the evening was perfect for shooting. Total bag, twelve and a half brace, eight hares, and a snipe. My share, six brace grouse and three hares. The

above is an unexaggerated statement of the grouse
sport that may be expected in Bute, with good
shooting, good walking, and good dogs. If any of
the three requisite *bons* fail, of course the bag will
be proportionally diminished.

I have never thought it worth while to take a
whole day at partridges, as all the arable land lies
in detached patches far apart from each other.
My plan has always been to divide the day
between black game and partridge. My first day
was on the furthest extremity of our shooting
beat. "September 14th.—Had a low game day on
Skirles and the fields of Clochnabae. Bag contained four and a half brace of partridges, two and
a half brace of black game, a grouse, three hares,
and a leveret." Two of the black game were old
cocks flying rapidly over my head at long distance.
This is generally counted a difficult shot, but it is
more properly a matter of calculation than difficulty. I found this out when a lad shooting wild
ducks at evening flight. Whenever a paired duck
and drake flitted overhead, the male, who always
yields precedence, invariably dropped, while his
mate in advance was certain to escape. Acting on

my discovery, habit and practice soon made the necessary distance-calculation quite natural, and now my first impulse on seeing any bird flying towards me is to note its speed and distance, and allow accordingly.

My second low game-day was to Robodach, a farm lying at the foot of the narrow part of the Kyles. Partridges have bred well there this year, and every autumn an enormous flock of tempting but unapproachable black game haunt the hill-side, feeding morning and evening on the corn stubbles. An unbroken heather-beat of six miles from Kames Castle ends in Robodach fields, so I shot along the moor edge to this partridge ground, killing on my way one and a half brace black game, a grouse, and three large red hares. After two o'clock, with fresh dogs, I increased my bag by four and a half brace of partridges and another couple of hares. Oddly enough, made the same score of partridges on both beats, and with the same number of shots, for I only missed a second-barrel bird each day.

Most of the Robodach partridges, when sprung, having found safety in the copsewood flanking the stubble and turnip fields, on my next

excursion to that ground I endeavoured to intercept the birds from their refuge. We were fortunate in forcing some good coveys into the hill-
ground, where I had fair shooting, and made a
score of eight brace—my largest partridge bag of
the season. In this low shooting the retriever
backed up the gun by securing winged birds all
but lost. Neither in wood, furze, turnip, nor
potatoes has one wounded partridge foiled this
invaluable dog since the shooting began.

But if the retriever did justice to the gun, the
gun, in its turn, did justice to the shooter. I have
never used a small fowling-piece that does more
unfailing, deadly execution. It was made by
Alexander Henry, of Edinburgh, a short time before the " Henry rifles " acquired their fame. I was
telling Henry of a duck gun made by his former
chief, Mr Ross (who then had a monopoly of the
Edinburgh gun trade), which for regularity of pattern and hardness of shooting I had never seen
surpassed. He answered by offering to make for
me a light gun to try against it, which I was to
return if not pleased. The stocking of this gun,
after the model of the Ross one, fitted me so well

that the first day I tried it in Mull I bagged 10½ brace of grouse (every bird I shot at), leaving off without a miss, and the very first brace of bagged birds were a fair right-and-left chance.

Although a number have died this year of disease, hares are still plentiful enough both on Kames and North Bute. We can generally each day kill as many as are convenient to carry, and rabbits are again on the increase, after being nearly exterminated by hired warreners a few years since. Alpine hares have been introduced from Argyllshire, but I have never yet moved one, although my watcher saw a couple at different times last winter, after they had donned the snow-white fur. I don't regret their scarcity, for on my last shooting they swarmed into a perfect nuisance. You could only shoot there in comfort by always giving them the cut direct when they rose, and most certainly by refusing to honour them with a gun salute. The pointers or setters soon learned to follow my example, and were as callous to the antics and vagaries of these hares as if they had been sheep. When the grouse began to fight shy of our advances, we were fain to scrape up acquaintance with the bluecoats—now putting on their wintry livery—and with the aid of terriers and retrievers could any day load a pony and his panniers with them.

It is the belief of some naturalist authorities that Alpine and Irish hares are of the same species, and that any apparent difference is caused by variation of climate. They maintain that, on the colder mountains of Scotland, the Irish hare would grow white in winter, while the Scotch white hare would retain the summer blue on the Irish plains during the severest December and January snows. From close observation of both, I entirely dissent from this theory. The Irish hare is thinner in the fur, which has a dash of red very different from the summer mouse-blue of the Scotch hare; the body is more lightly made for the limbs ; and having hunted them a whole season on the plains of Boyle, I can vouch for it that no Alpine hare would live before *foxhounds* half the time these Irish ones constantly do.

I have in my collection Alpine hares in summer and winter dress, together with an Irish one, and the difference is apparent to the most careless observer. I may also ask, why should not the mild air of Bute have prevented the two snowy specimens my watcher discovered from assuming their unsullied attire? White, in his ' Selborne,' records his satisfaction at the addition of the Alpine hare to the scanty animal catalogue of the British fauna, and would no doubt have protested against such summary swamping of it in the lineage of the Emerald Isle.

The same theory is broached with regard to our truly national red grouse and the willow grouse of Norway. Now, although there are strong points of resemblance both in the flight and summer plumage of the Norse bird to ours, there is this (to me) insuperable objection—viz., that no red grouse can exist without heather; and it also tells against the curtailers of species that the Scotch mountains should be cold enough to whiten [Irish (?)] hares and ptarmigan, and yet be too mild to perform the same office for willow grouse.

That hill partridges are distinct from lowland ones, which many sportsmen naturalists assert, cannot be so strongly supported; and I have always thought that the wilder feeding-ground of the moor-edge bird has only dwarfed the old English partridge, and somewhat darkened its feathers.

Mire-snipes are pretty generally distributed over the moorlands and waste ground of Bute, and a good sprinkling of jacks are constant to certain reedy plashes all through the winter. When killed off, their vacancies are generally not long in being supplied.* The boast of the island, however, is the woodcock. Last season was reckoned the worst woodcock year which the natives remember, while the preceding one was the best. Several of the shepherds assured me that, in the winter of 1864-5, there was not one for ten of the previous season, and yet, in comparison

---

* An old Argyllshire sportsman assured me lately that no retriever would carry a jack-snipe on account of their nauseous taste, of which the dog had the full benefit from being able to close its lips on the unsavoury morsel. Never having perceived this disgust to "jacks" in my retriever, I gave him a fair trial the first opportunity which occurred on my next shooting-day. I dropped the jack a good way off, loaded, and then desired the dog to fetch it. He carefully brought and laid it down at my feet, with every appearance of satisfaction and comfort. This is no doubt one of those retailed blunders which may pass muster long enough from not being challenged and proved false.

with much of the cover-shooting I have rented, the woodcock sport of 1864-5 in Bute was really superior. With the exception of one distant snap, and taking all chances as they came, I had the good hap to bag the first fourteen woodcocks I fired at last winter. When hard frost set in, the average bag was from three to five couple, besides a fair score of other game. In a really good woodcock year, I have little doubt ten or twelve couple might be bagged on one day by a superior shot.

The variety of the early winter shooting of the Kyles keeps excitement alive, and adds zest to the sport. My diary of the 21st of last November notes that my son and I killed grouse, blackcock, woodcock, wild duck, moorhen, rabbit, and roedeer. On the following Wednesday, the 23d, grouse, black game, partridge, woodcock, snipe, hare, and rabbit.

Flying overhead, or pitched among the marshes, large flocks of golden plover and curlews some-times give occasion for " a family shot." The former keep much among the higher hill-tops, while the curlews chiefly affect the waste ground close to the sea. Both breed freely on the Bute moors; and last summer, when a pair of curlews were screaming and dodging our path, my retriever made a sudden stop at my heel. On giving him leave, he coolly walked a little way and laid hold of what (from the commotion it made) I fancied a leveret. The prisoner, a young curlew, was delivered up to me unhurt, and nearly the size of its equally noisy parents.

A moor lochan, imbedded among the very peaks of the North Bute hills, is the chosen resort of moss ducks. The loch is about half a mile in circumference, and its situation so retired as to attract, in addition to the ducks, about a score of herons. On account of the bare flat banks, stalking is impossible; but even were it otherwise, the herons seem to have constituted themselves the sentries of the loch, and, taking post all round it, their telescope necks effectually stop all stealthy intrusion. One day, when grouse-shooting round this loch, I noticed that the sentinels were absent. Coupling my setters, and giving them in charge of a gillie, I managed, by great care and waste of time, to fire a random shot into the thick of the

flock when they flew. The chance was much too
distant to injure their bodies, but a duck and
drake dropped wing-broken into the water. Both
made several dives, and finally disappeared at
opposite sides of the loch.   Confident in the pains-
taking caution of Auk, I desired him to search the
bank, expecting a shot when the ducks rushed
from their hiding into the water; but at the first
round this experienced retriever found and secured both, without giving either the chance of
making a dash from their concealment, which the
slightest bungle on his part would have enabled
them to do.

Not long after I had my revenge on one of the
self-elected guardians of the ducks. Placing one
of my sons a little below the outlet, where the
flight, when disturbed, are apt to leave the fresh
water for the sea, I showed myself on the top of a
steep height on the opposite side. As soon as I
appeared the ducks knit together and took wing,
but flew past the ambuscade quite out of reach.
Like all very young sportsmen, the boy fired a
warning to the ducks to take it high when again
expelled from their city of waters. Now it hap-

pened that the herons were ranged like soldiers
along the loch at the foot of the peak where I had
attempted my strategy. Directly on hearing the
report they climbed the air, and I had just time
to cock one barrel and shoot a front-ranker; but
had both barrels been on full bend, I could as
easily have dropped his rear file with a second
shot. The bird happened to be a fine male, and,
for a heron, plump enough to prove that the Bull
Loch fishmarket was well stocked.

Another company of herons have haunted the
opposite extremity of my shooting-beat both last
season and this. Unlike their usual habits and
nature, these last frequent the bare hard moor,
and appear quite independent of loch, stream, or
even morass. Like their neighbours, they always
post "a look-out," but are much tamer than herons
usually are. To any fair and open passer-by they
give little heed; but the least appearance of scout-
ing instantly raises their neck or puts them to
flight. I suppose they feed at night, and only rest
on the moor. Since the railways began, several
heronries in the neighbourhood of the lines have
been deserted, and the refugees have settled on

the trees of more secluded districts. The old heronry at Gartshore was abandoned at the very time when the trees in the gorge of the lonely Glen-Fruin were appropriated by a colony of these birds.

With the exception of the never-failing mergansers fishing the shallow water of the coast, and a few waders on the shore, the seas around Bute seem to have no attraction for wild fowl. This neglect of the many sheltered bays and shallows of the island seems strange, but of all birds it may most emphatically be said of sea-fowl, "There is no accounting for taste."

Roes and partridges are far more numerous in South Bute than on the northern division of the island which I rent. The copses of the Kyles, which so often helped the partridges to foil us, always, however, harbour a sprinkling of these beautiful little deer. Not wishing to disturb them much last winter, we had only one hunt, when I killed a very fine buck with a splendid head, and my son a large doe, both in prime order. This year, when beating for black game, we stumbled on a pair of roes which had acquired such con-

fidence in this forbearance as scarcely to heed the
report of our guns.

The rod-fishing of Bute is confined to a few
moor lochs of moderate calibre ; there are no fishing streams deserving the name.

"THE roe, Captain Waverley, may be hunted at all times alike; for never being in what is called pride of grease, he is also never out of season, though it be a truth that his venison is not equal to that of either the red or fallow deer." Such is the stately Baron of Bradwardine's verdict on roes and their venison. And who would deny the conclusion when arrived at from such premises? If the roe is "never out of season," and "may be hunted at all times," and is never "in pride of grease," I fully agree with the Baron, that the vile trash which he calls "venison" is only fit for a dog-kennel. But then the "if"—there's the rub. I dispute his premises *in toto*, and therefore deny his conclusion. The roe may not be hunted at all times alike. The roe *is* out of season the greater part of the year. Roes *are* sometimes in pride of grease, and when shot in this state are superior venison to either red or fallow deer.

I am fully aware that most sportsmen and housekeepers will meet this assertion with a shake of the head, but I am prepared to prove that every season I rented Glenfalloch I shot several roe-deer as fat as good mutton; and in January 1861, the first year of my lease, my son and I killed three bucks within a few days whose kidneys were loaded with fat. Several people came on purpose to satisfy their curiosity as to the condition of these bucks, and all agreed that if they were not " in pride of grease," no deer ever could be.

Some people insist upon larding roe-deer venison with beef or mutton fat, while others assert that the only way to make roe-flesh tolerable is to stew it. When a roe is out of condition, stewing and larding may disguise it as food, just as the French cook, by the help of condiments, made his master eat his old slippers; but people who would so treat a roe haunch in prime order deserve never to have an opportunity of spoiling one again.

The condition of roes is far more precarious than that of either red or fallow deer. In some seasons very few good ones are killed at all. Some localities, too, seem much more adapted to fatten them than others. During a lease of three years at Glenfalloch, we killed 31 roe-deer, and of that number 12 were in first-rate condition. The last year of a former lease in Aberdeenshire, I killed 19 roes, and my son 5, but the best of these 24 did not equal the worst of the Glenfalloch dozen. What is stranger still, during the year that we killed most fat ones at Glenfalloch, my brother complained that out of a number killed by them, only 20 miles distant, there was not one really good roe.

Why the Glenfalloch roes were fatter than those on any of my other rented shootings, I never could discover; but if even there, and *at the height of the season*, good ones were so rare, no wonder that the majority of sportsmen and house-keepers have branded roe venison with the ill name that has hanged so many dogs. The haunches of all our prime roes are simply roasted, and I never saw any one partake of them who did not say they were the most delicate and delicious of all venison. My brother, who has both red and fallow deer in perfection, decidedly gives the palm to roe—*when in condition.*

From the Baron's other assertion, that " the roe may be hunted at all times alike," I differ more completely than about the quality of its venison. The usual autumn announcements that "—— brought down a couple of stags and a fine roebuck," or " several harts and a couple of roe-deer in fine condition," scarcely need comment. The deer are killed at *their* best time of year, and are, of course, as fat as they can be ; while the poor roes are massacred out of season, being simply carrion. Until they exchange the red hair for the mouse-coloured, they are only bags of bones covered by some dark dry flesh, with not a particle of fat. The summer coat begins to change for the winter one in September, being complete in November, before which time no roes should be shot. Red-deer harts, on the contrary, never come into prime order until they are divested

of the winter grey, and have assumed the rich red
of the sporting season.

When the woods are thick with leaves, it is
very difficult to force a roe into open ground at
all, but instinct also warns it not to come into
view when at its weakest state. Thus, whether
for sport or food, the roe should never be hunted
except for the short time they are, or ought to be,
in their prime; and if this rule is broken, they will
equally disappoint the hunter and the gourmand.

Roes shed their horns from the middle of December till January, and are then at their best.
They begin to fall off in February; and by the
beginning of March they are useless as food till
the next roe-hunting season in November.

There are two methods of hunting the roe, the
choice of either depending on the extent of the
woods and the nature of the country. In extensive, unbroken, and impervious woods, an old,
steady foxhound is indispensable to force them
into open ground and through the passes. Day
after day they will dodge about in these favourite
fastnesses; but unless the hunter thoroughly under-
stands the sport, and knows every pass and open

space of the forest, he will most probably come home each evening without having fired a shot. Should, however, the country be dotted over with small copses and belts of plantation, without one large wood to shelter them, hunting roe with a foxhound is totally impracticable, and if persevered in, most of the roe-deer will leave the ground altogether. When a good, steady hound finds the track of roe, he will stick to it for half a day; and the quarry, well knowing the futility of seeking concealment in the near coverts, makes for some distant retreat, not to return perhaps for weeks. For such small woods many people prefer beaters, but I have always observed that beaters, after the first few drives, shy the roes more, and make them more wary and cunning, than dogs do. I have also the objection to a noisy troop, that it is a lazy and stupid way of killing game.

The Glenfalloch coverts were chiefly oak copse, with a sprinkling of larch and fir. None of them being of great extent, and all tolerably open, pleasanter roe-shooting could not be had. There were no other guns than my son's and my own, and no other beating aid than one keeper and two re-

triever dogs. The retrievers were under perfect
command, and never were permitted to persecute
the roes needlessly, so the latter soon became ac-
customed to them, and, feeling confident of easily
eluding their pursuers even in these small coverts,
scarcely ever took the trouble to quit them.

In a larch plantation, close to our doors, a
couple of does lived all summer. The largest had
twins and the other a single fawn, which they
constantly brought within gunshot of the drawing-
room window; and when singing was going on,
would pause with great curiosity and apparent
pleasure. There could be nothing more beautiful
in nature than the fairy-like fawns frisking around
their graceful mothers, listening to the music in
rapt surprise.

After leaving Glenfalloch at the conclusion of
the autumn shooting and fishing, I always returned, accompanied by one of my sons, for a
fortnight's early and ten days' later winter sport.
Roes, of course, occupied a good deal of our attention, but woodcocks and wild-fowl had their full
share of the time. We generally arranged to beat
one or two of the smaller coverts before beginning

to range for winged game, but never, unless when
hunting the two larger woods on the opposite side
of the valley, gave a whole day to roe. Although
the river Falloch intervened between the woods
on the opposite and those on our side of the
valley, the old bucks and yeld does often crossed
backwards and forwards, but the younger bucks
and those does which had fawns at their feet never
left their own copse unless when hunted out.

On the first summer of my lease, when returning from fishing, I came suddenly upon a solitary
roebuck with horns of such length and thickness
as to excite both my wonder and admiration. The
keeper assured me he knew him well, having tried
hard the winter before to procure this famous head
for my predecessor in the game tenancy. I heartily congratulated him on his failure, and myself
that *my* turn was now come.

Our first winter campaign opened at Martin-
mas. We killed nine roes, and procured some
very good heads ; but *the head,* although several
times started, always contrived to elude us. As
was his habit, the wary old fellow kept much to the
steep, widespread patches and scattered clumps

on the opposite hill, where the approach of an enemy was readily seen and the means of escape various and easy.

The snows of 1861 came late, so the roes were at their best when we returned after Christmas to finish the shooting season. Three fell the first morning of our range—two of them old bucks, fat as venison should be, and neither had cast their horns. They were both (rare in roe-hunting) open, quiet chances. At first starting, I noticed a buck and two does on the bare hillside; but we knew, if they were properly moved, the direct path they would choose would be for the nearest copse. By taking a wide circuit, I gained the shelter of a brook commanding this sheep-track, while my companions got to windward of the deer a long way above.

I had my eye on the trio from the first; but although the drivers were directly in their wind, they showed no sign of uneasiness until the distance was much decreased. The buck then ceased feeding, and stood like a statue, while the does looked at him occasionally, but still kept nipping the grass. None of them seemed inclined

to quit the ground until the enemy actually came
in sight. They then knit together, and, led by
the buck, threaded their course leisurely down
the burnside. The near view of my game was,
however, obstructed by a mound, until the leader
presented himself within shot. From the first I
fully expected a right and left; but the does, on
hearing the noise, ducked back and took the hill
again, while the buck, making a magnificent six-
feet spring over the paling into the copse, fell
dead on the other side.

About two hours later my son sighted the
other buck feeding in a green open patch of an
oak coppice flanked by a wall, which enabled him
to secure an excellent still chance. His horns
were so loose that one of them was knocked off
when he fell.

With three roes in the larder on the first evening of our attack, we did not grudge a couple of
frosty days to woodcock, hare, snipe, and such
"small deer." On the fourth morning the keeper
and pair of retrievers again plied their arduous
work in the thickets. The dogs were thrown into
the first patch with no great expectation of rous-

ing a roe, but they soon feathered and opened, bringing round the quarry full before my hiding-bush. It was, as I fancied, an enormous doe ; and making sure that she must be in as prime order as the bucks last killed, I had great plea-sure in rolling her over. What was my disgust on walking up to find it was a buck, and to be convinced from his size and weight that he could be no other than the patriarch, whose antlers had been so often coveted, and which were now lying where he had cast them, as useless lumber, away. When this roe-deer was "gralloched," and an in-side disclosed like that of a summer wedder, we began to console ourselves that, though hornless, such "a buck in the hand" might be worth both him and his horns "in the bush" of next year. These were the three bucks before alluded to ; but during the last two seasons of my lease we killed not only some more bucks, but also four does, not a whit behind them in condition.

Although we had such good roe-shooting, there were only four right-and-left shots fired the whole time of our lease. Two of these doublets were distant chances, and fell to my share. Both times there were only a pair of roes; and in each case the first fell, and its neighbour, being badly wounded, was recovered shortly afterwards.

The other two double shots were fired by my second son. On the first trial he killed with one barrel; with the other he missed. Next opportunity, however, both roes dropt to shot.*

At this fortunate moment he occupied the highest pass on the opposite side of the Falloch, while my other son and I guarded the runs nearly in the line below him. Two large does and a buck crossed within fair range, and from the lower ground we distinctly noticed the pair drop, and the third come thundering down hill in a frantic manner. But its panic, by scaring it from its usual track, saved its life; for although the creature came within reach of the lowest gun, a hollow of the hill hid it at the critical time. The keeper and upper shooter soon after appeared with the buck and largest doe on their shoulders,

---

* I have known many old sportsmen who have shot roes all their lives, and yet never knocked over a couple right and left. During my whole shooting life I have only done so three times, and yet few men have slain more roes.

while the low pass gun bitterly complained of the unsocial habits of all roes that had challenged its powers, avowing that, barring the dignity of twin barrels, it might as well have been a single !

A small belt of tangled brushwood fringing the Arnan burn, interspersed with tall firs which had weathered the blasts of one hundred winters, is a favourite feeding-place of the Glenfalloch roes. Seldom more than a pair at a time lodged in this quiet retreat, but whenever they were killed off others supplied their room. As in most small plantations, the surest passes were at a little distance from the wood, and in this instance our object was to intercept them when making for the hill on their way to the next shelter. When flushed, they were almost sure to choose one of three retreats, but the two top escapes (about 100 yards apart) might with vigilance and activity be guarded by the same gun. Unless watched by eyes thoroughly used to the sport, the roes were almost certain to flit spectre-like into the burn track unperceived; in this case it was impossible to guess which of the two top escapes they would attempt, until too late to change should they

attempt the unguarded one. The quick and wary
eye of a practised roe-hunter seldom gave them
this advantage, and, watching every fall or rise in
the intervening ground where a passing glimpse
might be snatched, could with all but certainty
predict their course, and be ready to welcome
them with a salute. I had a particular fancy for
these two passes, and by means of a smart race
between them now and then, killed six roes, and
did not allow a single escape to the hills.*

Our last hunting-day at Glenfalloch was perhaps the most exciting and scientific I ever took
part in. We had already bagged 28 roes, and
were careless of shooting more, the day in fact
being intended for small game. The pair of larch
trees which spanned the Falloch, claiming equal
right with the celebrated Menai to the title and
dignity of bridge, had been safely crossed. Ben
Glass with its rugged face had been wellnigh
breasted, and I was thinking of the old " packman"
frozen to death a year before, and whose cairn with

---

* A woodcock was hiding within a few yards of the place
where one of these roes fell. It sprang when we were examining the dead animal, and was cut down by a roe charge.

a shred of his wretched clothes lay close at hand,
when my son gave the warning word "roes."
There were three in group, and a fourth at a short
distance from them. All were full grown, and
much of a size. Excepting a scanty sprinkling
of trees interspersed with occasional patches of
brushwood, the whole hill-face was bare, and appeared more so from a thick coating of snow. The
creatures seemed fully to comprehend the situation, and to know as well as we did how difficult
it would be to steal on them unperceived. Those
in company therefore went leisurely ahead, while
the single one deigned no further retreat than
to move a little on one side, so as to give us " a
wide berth" in passing him. Our game, by appear-
ing equally careless and *sang froid*, was to entice
them to slip quietly into some secluded hiding,
either among the alder bushes fringing the brooks
which seamed the mountain-side, or perhaps behind some cluster of hillocks, where by humouring the wind we could stalk them like deer.

As in all wild shooting, success depended entirely on our marking the next resting retreat of
the roes, without making them aware that we had

done so. It was, in fact, a fair trial, whether we or our game had the keenest eyes; for if the snow-tracks gave us a hint where to direct our survey, the fugitives were quite aware that we were hanging on their rear; and the three pairs of trained and skilful eyes scanning every rugged neuk of the forward ground, were well matched by three pairs as watchful and wary, noting every moving speck from behind, rendered more distinct by the weary waste of snow.

Twice the skulkers attempted concealment, their first retreat being found out by my son, and the second by myself. Both times, however, they had an eye on us first, and, instinctively warned by our bearing, moved on again with quiet and cautious step.

"They'll no stop noo till they get as far as the agle's nest forenent Corrynge," quoth the keeper, while we doggedly determined not to let them off while there was daylight.

This wood, a straggling patch of alder and hazel in the gorge of a rocky corrie where the eagle and raven built, was at the extremity of our shooting beat. There was still another stiff climb to it, so, despatching the keeper and retrievers to follow the course of the burn on the low side of the scrubwood, my son and I leisurely scaled the mountain for the high passes. We calculated that the keeper would require half an hour before getting to the far end of the wood, and fully an hour must elapse ere he could drive the roes forward to our passes on the near side. These passes were some hundred yards apart, and I was dreamily sauntering to mine when I stumbled on the tracks of our game. In a moment I saw they were shirking the wood, and evidently bent on topping the mountain, most likely with the intention of regaining their former ground. A more cunning manœuvre could not have been planned, and had it not been for the tell-tale snow, it would have been completely successful.

Briskly following up "the spoor" to the first fair look-out, I soon detected the three resting at the high corner of the wood, but without having entered it. They were as yet distant, but their still watchfulness, and the equality of the ground, made it impossible to stalk them. To my surprise and pleasure a low whistle from the adjacent height revealed my son's head peering also at the roes. He had noted my change of course, and at once suspecting the cause, had actually seen our game before I did. There now seemed a fair prospect of success, for by placing him above on the outer shoulder of the hill, and creeping on them myself from below, the deer would be very likely to cross within reach of the high gun.

During the whole time these hunting tactics were going on, the roes, with the exception of turning their heads now and then to look and listen, kept perfectly motionless, and I was first made aware that my comrade had turned their flank by the united eyes and ears of the listeners being raised in the same direction. Instantly aware of their danger, they marched with deliberate caution round the base of the hillock on the other side of which was the gun, and again were safe from the snare. Sharper-eared than Indians, they had heard stealthy footsteps on the crusted snow, and fairly circumvented them by this masterly double. The snow which had revealed them made amends by being the abettor of their escape, and it seemed as if the white carpet spread on the mountain by the skies disdained to have its purity sullied by the red blood of the victims of its own betrayal.

Scarcely had the three roes flitted from the high ground above me, when the keeper and retrievers rose from the hollow underneath. His hawk eye had caught a glimpse of the guns on the hillside, saw that we avoided the passes, and, profiting by this discovery, he had followed in the wake, until he too perceived the cause. Unable, however, to find out our plan of approach, he had prudently kept himself and dogs in hiding until the deer made their wary exit.

A better illustration of the power to compel success which knowledge of the sport gives the roe-hunter, I have seldom had the pleasure to record. Here were three men left entirely to their own resources, and none of them made the slightest mistake. At parting, they all made sure that their game had taken shelter in the wood. These deer at first were half a mile distant from the nearest gun, and yet all three hunters, though far separated, detected them and marked their last dodge, while they themselves had no idea that even one spy had witnessed their cunning.

The short winter day was fast wearing out, but the pursuers' hopes were as strong as ever. The roes had been scarcely able to feed all the forenoon, and no doubt felt confident that the last clever trick on the hill peak had fairly entitled them to a supper. We were therefore quite convinced that they would settle to the evening meal at the first convenient halting spot.

Giving his gun to the keeper, my son scouted forward with a telescope, and from screen of rock or tree scrutinised the hidling corries or scrubby patches which might possibly shelter our game. Crawling on hand and knee to the pinnacle of a wide look-out, we saw his attention fixed. Up goes the glass, to remain steady for a few seconds, when it was shut up with a satisfied jerk, and he descended on all-fours. Before a word was spoken I felt sure the chase was at length happily safe.

The three roes were greedily eating among some stunted birches skirting a mountain brook, and from the direction of the wind and lay of the feeding-ground could not have been more aptly

placed. Leaving the keeper with dogs and telescope on the top of the mound, the shooters
mapped out so wide a flank movement as to
prevent the possibility of being either seen or
winded by the quarry, now at last careless and
secure.

The various eccentric turns and doubles of our
game had again placed us close to the spot where
we first found them at noon, and with so fair a
prospect of coming to close quarters at the end
of the day, no wonder that the fourth unsociable
buck was quite overlooked. Scarcely had we
quitted the keeper and dived for concealment
among the rugged peaks and scaurs of the mountain face, when " the solitary " burst from his lair
among the whins right athwart our course, but
scarcely had he got into his stride when a shot
from my son's gun paralysed the fleet limbs that
had almost saved him, and, rolling over the crag,
he lay powerless at its foot.

Our first act was to cast an eye on the look-
out. There he was, steady as the rock he leaned
on, neither the shot nor the fall of the roe having
slackened for an instant his attention from the

watch we had set him. Our deer was soon despatched, cleaned, and hung on the nearest tree.
We then pointed in the direction of the birches.
A nod from the scout gave confidence to our
stalk, being a well-understood signal that the trio
had not been moved by the shot.

Thoroughly acquainted with the ground, the
younger sportsman took position on line, but
considerably beyond the birches where the deer
were feeding, while the elder took advantage of a
hillock about a hundred yards below, and close to
the burn scaur.

A slight motion of my cap warned the keeper to
come on. He first slipped out of sight for a little
time, and began to whistle and speak to his canine
accomplices, gradually emerging, as if accidentally,
into view, having exactly the appearance of a shepherd "wearing" his flock. Dozens of times we
well knew the roes had witnessed this operation,
and were quite callous to it, so when the man
now wheeled to the right, then to the left, but
always nearing them as if by chance, the creatures were as easily herded as three " harvest
hogs." They strayed slowly down the burn, and

I was first aware that they were close upon my hiding-place by a head peering over the mound within pistol-shot of the muzzle of my gun. Anxious for a right and left, I was loath to fire until the three had topped the hillock, so the rejected head caught sight of its contemner, and ducking back warned the others, when they all scampered away.

I was on the hillock top in an instant, but an unfortunate dip in the ground hid them until nearly out of reach, when I fired and struck the rear one bounding straight from me. At full pitch of their speed, the now terrified creatures dashed past the high gun, a long cross-shot. The leader fell dead, but the others, scared anew, swerved down hill, only allowing the second barrel time for a distant snap at the one I had before struck. The pair rushed down the burn's bank, one of them crossed, and immediately showing on the other side, darted up the hill at full stride; why the other lagged behind, we were at no loss to guess.

There was no dispute about the lurking-place of the wounded roe. Without a word we at once

begun the search, and found him at the very spot
we anticipated. He was standing sideways at 70
yards from my feet, when I fired and dropped him
on his side. He rose, and struggling down the
steep, was quickly pulled down by my favourite
retriever.

The dusk was now merging into darkness, the
chase having lasted from high noon till past five
o'clock. Weary and hungry, with a heavy roe
slung upon each of our shoulders, and a long,
rough, dark journey home, I will nevertheless
make bold to assert that a more "heartsome" or
merrier one never was taken.

After the many splendid roe-hunts I have followed, both in former and in later years, it is my
firm conviction that gun-fanciers can only under-
value this sport from lack of knowledge. No
doubt deer-stalking is both interesting and exciting to a tyro even from the first. He has the
whole open panorama spread before him, and a
sort of hazy, mystified conception of the plan of
operations. Above all, he is encouraged by the
stalker (in whose hands he is a mere puppet) with
the probability, nay almost certainty, of a fair rifle

shot at a noble hart. Very different is the pursuit of the roe. The shooter is, *or ought to be*, left to his own unaided powers, and many a blunder will he perpetrate, and many a hard day's work undergo, before he acquires the skill to warrant success. Confidence, of course, grows in proportion to the skill, but many sportsmen give up heart ere they have gained either, and naturally stigmatise " the following of the roe" as " dull work," and point perhaps to the few wretched specimens they have slain out of season as evidences that roes are equally unsatisfactory both when hunted and on the table.

I have been assured by a Fife proprietor that roes are migratory in the border counties. They come down, he said, from the Highlands in numbers during severe weather, returning to their hills again when the storms abated, exactly like deer. In my Highland shootings, however, I never noticed any decrease of roes when the winters were at their roughest; and had there been an exodus from my woods I must have perceived it, as I always knew well before Christmas what roe-deer were on the ground.

AUTUMN ANGLING ON THE LYON.

WHEN tenant of the shootings of Garth, in Perth-shire, in the summer of 1858, I had obtained leave, through the interest of my kind landlord with the liberal proprietor, to fish salmon over nearly the whole of the river Lyon. The privilege, so freely accorded, was no common boon; for, in addition to the high rate at which salmon angling is now held, this river flowed through a singularly picturesque district of oak-wood, moorland, and mountain, while the well-separated and finely-defined pools gave ample scope for a full and powerful cast.

As comparatively few of the larger fish ascended the higher waters of the Lyon, I seldom wandered above the heavy streams, where the best salmon,

when in the river, were sure to lodge. The upper
stretch was, however, to many, the more tempting
half; for, in addition to the romantic scenery, each
good pool or stream teemed with keen and lively
grilse.

Garth House was about six miles from the
nearest upper salmon pool of the beat. The remaining ones, at longer or shorter distances from
each other, extended some miles higher. After
them, a stretch of very moderate water ended in
the fine grilse casts above Meggerny Bridge.

When the days were long and fine, the walk
along the Lyon's banks and braes was wonderfully
pleasant, but towards the " hint o' hairst," as the
weather began to break and the light early to fail, a
small spring-cart and pony, hired from the "general
merchant," added much to the comfort, and, by
saving time, even to the success of a salmon day.

Tommy, the pony, a fat strawberry dumple, and
his driver, a stout lad of fourteen, had a perfect
sympathy with each other's feelings and failings.
Both were squat, good-tempered, selfish, shrewd in
economising trouble, and pre-eminently lazy. To
do Danie justice, he was a sagacious monkey, his

intense love of country gossip having even a slight
smack of the antiquary; and, in truth, the drive
up Glenlyon afforded a fair field for his imagination and memory. From the gushing waterfall
on Chesthill Brae, with its mouldering brig, the
ruinous tower of Carnibarn, the old Popish kirk-
yard, the eleven elm-trees—called, if I remember
rightly, "The Daughters of Glenlyon," and which
formerly did duty as milestones—to the fat farmer,
within a trifle of 7 feet, whose weight turned a
beam of 30 stone, Danie had always subjects for
our admiration—or wonder!

Three weeks of warm July days had dwindled
the Lyon to a thread when I saw it first, and on
asking a resident on its banks his opinion of its
angling capabilities, I received the following *very*
encouraging reply—"Oh! you mustn't expect to
do great things; but if it comes a fresh, there's
one pool where you *might* get a fish, if you were
getting up at two o'clock in the morning." Pleasant prospects!

An almost uninterrupted succession of dry sunny
weather still kept down the river until the Lammas
floods. When the water was slightly swelled by

a few refreshing showers, only some of the deeper pools came into low trim, quickly falling back again to their thin clear state. The Garth keeper, however, being well acquainted with the upper water, and also having a good idea both of the size and colour of the salmon flies, no time was lost, when the clouds now and then grudgingly favoured us with their driblets. Long before they were needed, I had tied, by the light of the glorious July sun, every variety of summer and autumn salmon fly that the river in its most exacting state could demand.

A previous day and night of rain brought the keeper at the end of the month to say there was "plenty water." On running down to the river-side it was too thick and drumly for fly, and an old roadman volunteered the advice that "she was ower big for fishing." Better too big than too small, thought I; so the casts for to-morrow were carefully arranged, with rod, gaff, and bag ready at a moment's notice.

Next morning we were off for the high pools at eight o'clock, in spite of a hazy atmosphere and drizzling rain. While plodding past the first clachan, a shoemaker said something in Gaelic to a knot of gossips around him. "What's that, Mac?" "He jist says, sir, we may turn aboot hame, for ye might as weel throw a flee on the hee-road as on the Lyon the day."

I am afraid this well-meant hint did not produce the effect intended, but very much the contrary. Our only reception of the prophecy was to march defiantly up the brae.

The first pool, a long and likely one, I swept over with great caution. Few anglers, indeed, begin to fish carelessly; but it is the test of a skilled hand that his patience and wariness never fail, and so he is never taken by surprise at the sudden bolt of a royal fish. Genuine and spurious anglers may readily be distinguished by the calmness and temper of the former in working a difficult river, where fish are scarce and hard to move; while the latter soon lose heart, and before the day is half over fairly give in. Fishers of this last stamp may be keen enough when fish are numerous, and on the rise; but it is only the gifted few who, after a long and barren day, will deliver their first and final casts with equal vigour and precision.

Not a fin stirred in this promising bit of water
to my crow-wing fly, neither did a dark mottled
turkey feather prove more alluring. A white trout,
however, rose in the pool above. Mac, who was
apt to be sanguine, affirmed it was a grilse; but
we could not decide the point, as it refused to show
again.

The next two casts were my special favourites.
They are considerably apart—one, flowing close to
the road, is deep, confined, and eddying; the other,
half a mile upward, gave scope for one of those
splendid sweeps of the line which is the delight
of the salmon angler's heart. But, alas! changes
of dark flies did not even excite a contemptuous
"bell-up." The lighter lures of grey turkey-wing,
and brown hackle, and argus-wing with red
hackle, only fixed three yellow trout about half a
pound each, which, instead of being welcomed, did
but disgust me with light flies for the rest of the day.

I had now carefully searched every pool and
stream to the top of the beat, without one break
of a salmon. There remained only time to skim
over a few pet casts on the return—our last chance
of cheating the brogue-maker's spell. The free

upward pool, where the yellow trout were so officious, had been twice tried with varied lure. It had scarcely rested an hour, still I could not resist a third attempt with the crow-wing. At the throat of the stream, where I had so shortly before taken especial pains with this same fly, up came the salmon, sucked down the hook, and was firm and fast. It made a fine run, and when landed was nearly 10 lb., and clear as silver.

The homeward water was tried with equal pains and change of fly, but there was not another offer all day. In passing the cottages the shoe-maker prophet of evil met us on the road with " Whaur's the salmon?" in English. Mac, who espied him at a distance, had slyly slung the bag out of sight. He replied, with a grin, " In the bag," and nodded over his shoulder. " So ye hae," was the rejoinder; "atweel, I wudna hae thocht."

In some rivers, such as Spey, where salmon are constantly moving, the second fisher has nearly as good a chance as the first, and a man may often hook a salmon in a pool which shortly before he had drawn blank. Such rivers, how-

ever, are rather the exception than the rule, and
in by far the greater number of salmon streams,
after the water has been searched by an able
angler, his successor's prospects are considerably
blighted. On my next fishing day, however,
I had the satisfaction of picking up the worm
from before the very beak of a "two o'clock in
the morning" bird.

A close and sultry air made the whole *genus
salmo* quite as stubborn as on my first introduction to the Lyon; and although I swept the water
leisurely up to the stream where I killed the
salmon a few days before, the only offers were
the splash of a playful grilse which declined to
continue the game, and the fix of a really good
river-trout which slipped off.

On reaching the bank of my fortunate pool,
the sun opportunely glanced on the brass reel
belonging to an uncouth rod, evidently hid in
a hurry among the rank grass. A pair of hob-
nail boots peeping out from under "the busses,"
as Mac calls the whins, quickly revealed the
owner of the rod, and we unkennelled the comical
old "Bellman," who shammed a nap to perfec-

tion. He had been out since the dawn, he said, but "hadna steered a fin" or seen a fish "a' day." To punish old Slyboots, a fine salmon floundered up at this moment before us, as if to give him the lie direct. The confusion on "Belltow's" face and the smirk on Mac's were rare fun. He saw at once that the old man had not only seen this fish, but (as we afterwards were told by the Meggernie keeper was fact) had most likely thrown over it, and was " waiting on" for another trial when he heard our approach. His tactics, then, were to hide himself; and if found out, to feign sleep, but at all events to conceal from us that there was a *feeding salmon* in the pool.

Taking post about twenty yards above the fish, I threw cautiously over him with my dark fly, and at the first free sweep he sprang beautifully and fastened. He first struck across the stream, and then made some fine bursts up and down the pool before I could tire him. In the thick of it I heard the old man's "Gie't line, Gie't line," to which, of course, I paid no respect, and Mac vainly trying to keep him quiet. When gaffed, this salmon proved a 12-pounder, and fresh from the sea.

N

The bellman had no less than three flies on his cast, only about a foot apart! But even had they been well separated, or fished with singly, none of them, I am convinced, would have had much chance of hooking a Lyon salmon.

The hot day and hard work made a draught from the spring at the nearest farmhouse very delicious, and the luxury of "a drink" is enhanced by sucking it through our "*patent*" drinking-horn —the hollow bone of a roe's foreleg.

Sunning himself close to the spring, a stone-blind man was making pirn-lines in the most dexterous manner I ever saw. He also had a little workshop, and coopered pails, "bowies," &c., remarkably well. I bought a trout-line from him as a curiosity, and a neat "cogue" to water the pony with from the roadside burns. This blind man supports himself in comfort even in a lonely Highland glen.

The last fishing-day with Mac was unfortunate. At the tail of the first pool, hitherto a barren one, I hooked a salmon. It was lost entirely by Mac missing his first gaff, and being too nervous to take advantage of a second chance, after which the fish broke its hold. Had four more rises in different pools, but no fastens, although I spared neither time nor change of lure to effect one. A fine sky and good water, but fish rose shyly, and only nipped at the fly.

August was nearly ended, the weather settling again after the floods, and river getting small. From the scanty water there were only two pools I had much trust in, so I paid them a stately visit in the "general merchant's" equipage. In one of these pools I sprang a fish five times, fixing him at the fifth offer, and losing him from being tenderly hooked. In the other I killed a small fish of 6 lb., but very clean and handsome.

After a tract of fine harvest-days the skies overcast, and weather broke into continued heavy rain. The first fair morning I rode up the glen alone on the lazy strawberry cob, and found the water in good large ply. I had scarcely wetted my line before the clouds gathered, and poured down their bucketfuls. The river soon began to wax, which of course kept down the fish, although I tried the best casts with large and likely flies.

Expecting a friend to dinner, and time being

nearly "up," I was giving a closing sweep to the
tail of "the road pool" before trotting home, when
at this *malapropos* moment a splendid salmon
hooked! The casting-line being only fine single gut,
the first touch of my fish proved that, to land him,
he must be worked for with patience and caution.
From the roughness and steepness of the bank,
the safest although most tedious course was, if
possible, to prevent the monster from leaving the
pool. As he proved "a sulker," there was little
difficulty in detaining him, but his phlegmatic
temper was such a stress on mine as sorely to
tempt me to risk my vantage-ground in the fight,
when two farm-hinds who had been watching from
a distance walked deliberately down to the opposite bank, and set themselves doggedly to see it
out. All thoughts of hurrying the salmon, at the
risk of the light tackle, were now given up. My
friend might be hungry, and the dinner spoiled,
but the gaping clodpoles should never see me
break my fish.

After nearly two hours' wary work, the victim
became so weak and docile as to allow itself to
be guided to the bank. The sight of the white

gravel, however, always roused its ebbing energies to dart again into the deep. At every dash away from the shore, the laugh of the onlookers was hearty and undisguised, until at last I shut them up by stranding a beautifully-shaped 16-lb. salmon on the sloping shingle.

My ride home would have been lengthy, had I not applied the only incentive to diligence Tommy respected—viz., a sharp spur. His master used to boast that he never tired or fell off in condition. This panegyric always reminded me of a lazy "minister's man" whose master had turned him off for this fault alone. The minister (who assured me he "would not tell a fib for all the world"), having occasion to be from home the week before the term, knew that his factotum would do literally nothing when he was absent, unless he bribed him with a good character. He therefore wrote in large text the words, "Sober, honest," &c., and wound up by "he gives sure evidence of being a very durable servant"—double-dashing the last three words. "The man" was delighted with his certificate, particularly the compliment at the end, promised to do all justice to

the glebe till his master's return, and kept his
word.

My friend met me at the door of Garth House,
accepted the fish as sufficient apology for my late
return, admired it to my heart's content, and expressed his determination (as he had never seen
a salmon landed) to accompany me on the next
fishing-day.

On the 13th of September the spring-cart was
early at the door. Including charioteer Danie,
we were a party of five, to Strawberry Dumple's
intense disgust, who firmly held with the doctor,
when ordered to swallow a box of his own pills,
that "one of us was a dose" up Glenlyon brae.
He evidently seemed to think our unwonted
weight a bitter pill; and both he and his master
tacitly agreed to walk all the way, unless when
we coaxed them into a shambling amble now and
then *down hill*.

As our friend wore thin shoes, and the walk
from the cart to the first pool was damp, we agreed
that I should try it alone, and the party drive on
and wait for me at the road pool, about a quarter
of a mile farther forward. Hitherto I had been

unfortunate in this pool, having lost the only fish I ever moved in it. This time, however, a heavy salmon rushed up at the tail of the stream and hooked firm. He made a noble spurt to begin— then bored up rapids—struck across river—sulked, and played all his tricks and vagaries. After an hour's severe play, he managed, in spite of me, to roll over the waterfall into the pool below. Still through this danger I kept him safe, and was in the very act of raising his unresisting head on the gravel when his well-worn hold parted! With a languid plunge he vanished amid the foam, and I rejoined my companions with a malediction on that "unchancy" pool.

The account of my mishap whetted our guest's appetite to witness the mysteries of a salmon-run. Each stream and pool to the top of the beat was, however, a failure, not even the excitement of a rise rewarding my labour and his patient watching. On the return I could evidently see that my friend's interest in the sport was gone, and his attention had quite flagged. A graceful bend of the river, or sudden rise of the opposite hill—the white clusters of the hazel or coral berries of the

rowan-tree—each in turn had far greater attraction for the contemplative man than perpetual
lashing for salmon who treated all our overtures
with silent contempt.

For the second time we pulled up at my favourite "road pool," but a prolific hazel copse had
tempted all our party under its shade, save one
who held my gaff. At the very top of the eddy,
and to the first throw, up bolted a salmon. It
made some fine rushes, then suddenly tamed, and
was easily "clipped." A small clear fish of seven
pounds. A short tract of dry weather again
lowered the Lyon. Before another "fresh" our
friend had left us, and to this day has never had
the satisfaction of "being in at the death" of
a salmon.

Close-time of this season seemed to have been
considerably anticipated by settled dry weather.
For the last few days that remained, rain appeared
hopeless in the face of a high barometer. I had
contentedly put up my fishing-gear till next year,
when a sudden and unexpected drenching rain
caused a fine flow of the river. Danie and I were
of course off betimes for the high water, and the

"unchancy" pool surrendered a first victim. It was only 6 lb., but, being body-hooked, made as sporting a run as many a fish triple its weight. Rose another in the "road pool," which declined to move a second time, and then drove to the long free stream below the blind man's house. On remarking to Danie that our line-making machine was absent from his settle at the gable of the house, he naïvely answered, "I see'd him *looking* oot o' his window."

The long stream is delightful fishing, pleasant even when one does not see a fish. On this fine angling day I cautiously tried the confined current at its top, and carefully raked the swirling eddies of the opposite bank, but it was not until the broadening waters at its close demanded the full pitch of an angler's powers that a beautiful salmon sprang. When fixed, he rolled round and round on the surface, lashing the water with his tail. After he got down I wondered at the want of energy and pluck in so good a fish, for before ten minutes' play he came sweetly to bank on his broadside. Danie held the gaff, and in his eagerness ran down to the salmon. "Now take time,"

quoth I, "and clip him true the first trial." Judge
my horror when the urchin seized the instrument
in both hands, and came down upon the salmon's
body as if he meant to fell an ox! Of course
the fish sweltered into the stream again, and the
wonder was that Danie's savage onslaught had not
snapped the line. Soon, however, the monster
came floating in sideways again, when, disarming
my ally of his weapon, I gaffed it myself. The
monkey came grinning up, without apology or
shame, shouting merrily, "I never see'd the like
o' that afore." The fish weighed 13 lb., and was
so quickly overcome from having, in the first
struggle, twisted the gut round its gills, and thus
drowned itself.

My two last angling-days of the Lyon having
now really come, I determined, by being early at
the lowest pool, to make the most of them. It
was forestalled, however; and a precautionary survey disclosed a brother of the craft, who had come
to grief by breaking his line. He was seated
mending his tackle, totally unconscious of my
discovery, and most likely before he was set up
again his rival was out of sight with a clear lead

of the water. But this sharp practice availed little, for not a fish showed until I got to the stream above "the wooden brig," the highest cast of our salmon-beat. There I moved a dark old fish three times. He began by a free dash at my black fly, then refused. Rested him some time, and tried him with a lighter; but only a head appeared this time. Another rest, and refusal of same fly, so gave him a brighter lure still. This last was only noticed by a sluggish "bell." Waited some time, changing flies and resting; but when salmon spring briskly at first, and become duller each succeeding rise, they are very apt, as in the present instance, finally to refuse altogether. When, on the contrary, the first rise is lazy, and the second more active, look sharp for the third offer, and take it coolly. The spin of the pirn-line will most likely prove its pleasing sequel!

On the return, not even a white trout stirred until I regained the low pool, which my alert Waltonian brother had already skimmed. A sly peep at an angler in difficulties, however, has generally an effect on his successor to the pool the very reverse of a damper. Heedfully, therefore, the rough sharp stream was fished down till it deepened and steadied, when a heavy fish followed the fly with one of those sweeping rolls deemed by many knowing anglers a hint that in their case rest time between the casts is superfluous ceremony. Instantly clapping the fly again before the salmon's nose, a furious rush and tightened line proved that I had read him right. He never sulked nor parleyed, but fought bravely on, doing his best to break his chain. A game customer like this is soon subdued, and in less than twenty minutes a 12½-lb. harvest fish lay gasping on the grass. During the struggle I twice saw its paired neighbour feeding in mid stream; and whenever I had cut the hook from the dead fish's jaw, I offered it to the lively relict in the pool. It came at once, but hooked so tenderly that one dash parted the slight catch.

Although I did not land a fish, the final day of the Lyon has left as pleasing reminiscences as any of its predecessors. A balmy morning and dry road tempted me to steal "cannily" up the glen on foot, more to enjoy a peaceful farewell of the now

familiar river than with much hope of hooking a
fish in water so thin and clear.

When I sauntered down to the first pool, I
found Chesthill's fisherman giving it the finishing
touches ; and he told me that another well-known
Lyon angler had had "his wull o't" shortly before,
but nothing had moved to either of them. The
tiny state of the river was warrant enough for
" ill luck," and I had turned away to seek some
of the deeper linns which might not have been
already raked, when the man begged me to try
this pool once more. "Three times was canny,"
and although they had "dune naething, he would
like weel to see't cuisten owre by me."

To please him, I put on my lightest tackle and
threw right across to the farther side with a long
and even sweep. Near the tail of the pool the
heaviest water runs close to the opposite bank.
This was the critical bit, as both the fisherman
and I knew full well. To fish it properly required
a most powerful throw, and yet from the still
clear state of the water the fly ought to fall like
gossamer. At the second attempt of this difficult

cast, a large red-tinged salmon fearlessly came
and hooked. Quickly shortening the line by
getting opposite his head, I thought I had my
captive safe, when he suddenly vaulted a foot
clear of the river and shook himself free. A
spectator and witness *is* a comfort when a heavy
fish *breaks its hold*, perhaps not when it breaks
the casting-line!

Moved two more salmon in the long pool below
the blind man's house, and touched one of them
sharply at second rise, but his neighbour refused
to come again. Nevertheless, from the scanty
water and bright sky, I had reason to be satisfied
that any fish deigned to notice my fly on the
last Lyon day of 1858.

Perfect contentment with a few salmon-rises
and an empty fishing-bag, by way of finale to an
angling season, can hardly fail to suggest "the
glorious nibble" of a brother enthusiast. Moving
large fish, however, is held by every true angler
only second to hooking them; but many persons
are apt to despise the most skilful and patient
efforts unless crowned with immediate success,
and to such the plaintive wail of an old craftsman

(when asked what he had caught) may suggest no unworthy moral—" *Nothing but twigs!*"

A popular periodical has lately been giving instructions on fish-culture, which to a Highland salmon angler are more amusing than instructive. Our first lesson is to follow the example of a careful gamekeeper, and trap all the vermin. These are pike, perch, eels, and the common river-trout. The vermin trap is a small-meshed net, to be used "in season or out of season while there is a head of vermin to be caught."

Now, it happens that almost all our best northern salmon streams, far from breeding pike, perch, and eels, are very indifferent for trouting. Their channels, being sharp and gravelly, are not adapted for these (vermin?) fish. It is only in the Don, the Tweed, and some of the more sluggish rivers flowing through pastoral districts, that even good yellow trout thrive. Only export perch, pike, and eels into the rapid and rocky northern waters, and a precious life they would lead!

But our periodical is also very urgent on the

artificial breeding of salmon. "Let us suppose," it argues, "that we have a river with a gravelly bottom, but destitute of fish of any kind. Let us further suppose that we stock it with twelve thousand salmon ova, and then leave it to take its chance. Something like the following results would ensue:—The ova would hatch in April or May; very shortly fish of prey would make their appearance," &c. Now, in place of "supposing" that "fish of prey would make their appearance" soon after the introduction of salmon into this formerly lifeless river, I firmly believe that even the salmon smolts themselves, like the Caithness nightingales, would never return after the first migration.

In Australia, where the salmon are forced to come back to some one of the rivers of that country or perish in the sea, it may be different, but any river of this country communicating with the sea, and destitute of salmon, grilse, or sea-trout, will remain so if there were twenty breeding-ponds on its banks.

I have not fished the Tay since the establishment of the Stormontfield ponds, but I think

I shall be borne out by the ablest Tay anglers in asserting that all the trouble and expense of salmon-breeding has not yet been followed by a corresponding increase of salmon.

The essayist I have referred to, however, "hits the clout" with his last arrow. "We cannot," says he, "quit the subject without alluding to the stake and bag nets used for the capture of salmon on the sea-coast."

Now, here is the gist of the whole matter. We had plenty of fine salmon in our rivers before the dexterity of the netters—especially of the sea-netters—thinned and dwarfed them. Just in proportion as restrictions are laid on the net, will all the trouble and expense of fish-culture and river protection have fair play. Many of the larger fish are so scared by the constant succession of net apparatus, as never to ascend beyond the heavy dead water at the foot of our rivers. In the estuary of northern Dee, some time since, a salmon was netted of 42 lb. weight, while none had been caught in that stream so heavy as 25 lb. for years before. Forty seasons ago, 30-lb. fish were frequently taken with the rod in that

river, and the journal of a Dee angler of those
days contains an entry of three fish between
20 lb. and 30 lb., taken out one after the other
from the same pool, *and on the same morning.*
Ask any Dee angler how many 20-lb. fish are
captured with the rod in a whole season now!*

Sea-netted salmon are in the finest order for
the table.   After ascending fresh water they
remain in good condition till the close of the
season; but the test of a first-rate fish is when
the sea-lice prove him fresh from the brine.   No
wonder, then, that sea-caught fish are in the
highest demand; and it is the exceeding skill
acquired by the sea-fishers in entrapping the very
salmon—as they strive to penetrate and stock
our rivers—that has done more to spoil salmon
angling than either breeding - ponds or river-
watching will ever be able to remedy.

---

* In 1855, from the 6th of March till the 15th of May, I
landed fifty-five, and my eldest son (then a lad at school) four
salmon on the Dee. He was only down for a short time now
and then, but had the good hap to kill a beauty of 21 lb.—the
heaviest clean salmon taken with the rod on our stretch of
waters for many seasons before. My largest fish was 18 lb.

A PTARMIGAN DAY.

ON the west coast of Scotland the very name ptarmigan implies loneliness and grandeur. In the north, where, from the greater prevalence of green stony ground, the birds become far more numerous, and the hills that allure them are more easily climbed and travelled, the association of this lonely denizen of the rocks with our sterner scenery is to some extent weakened. But on the western chain of the Grampians the very mountains themselves would lose caste both in romance and sublimity were their summits deserted by the alpine grouse.

So inaccessible are the breeding-places of the white grouse in the Western Highlands of Scotland, and so scanty is the stock of this game, that, always excepting shepherds, few of the natives have seen, and some never even heard of, such a bird.

"Ptarmigan ground" is therefore a most appropriate title for the magnificent cluster of mountains at the head of Loch Lomond, where every bald and rugged peak, capped with snow or shrouded in mist for half the year, has always nevertheless a scanty sprinkling of these lovers of desolation and contemners of the storm.

In these regions the very valleys and thoroughfares are lonesome and dreary; and despite the crowd of summer tourists that throng its banks, the otter fearlessly threads the Falloch when travelling between Lochs Lomond and Dochart. Sometimes, when watching the twilight flight of ducks, I have been startled by his peculiarly modulated whistle in the still bends of the river; and a detached rock close to the highway is known as the "otter's inn," from his resting a day there when changing his fishing-quarters.

The numerous detached heaps of rock and stone scattered along the hillsides, or grouped in fantastic outline on the brow, are each occupied by a family of discreet badgers, whose use-and-wont title is never disturbed, except when the mountain fox in spring takes forcible possession of the lower cairns, where the abundant stock of blue hares affords her voracious litter an unfailing supply.

Few, however, of the badgers' tenements are now challenged or required by his supplanting rival, for trap and gun are telling on the hill fox, and, like the marten and wild-cat, he is gradually becoming more rare. Still the old-fashioned "foxhunter" is not yet banished from these primeval lands, but conducts his spring and autumn hunts in the stereotyped style of "sixty years since."

He is a dark bony man in the decline of life, descended from a race of foxhunters, his father and grandfather having had charge of the same wild district as himself. Scrupulously polite and courteous to gentlemen — when addressing me he always gives the honour of knighthood—if irritated by the farmers or shepherds composing his hunt, he is a perfect master of Gaelic slang. Being a good running shot, he is as punctilious in claiming precedence for the first chance at a fox as the chief of the olden time at the stag; and woe betide the subordinate who dares to fire before him! Two farmers having bolted Reynard with their terriers from some rocks, and missed him just when the "tod-hunter" was rushing up, he saluted them with such a volley of abuse as completely stunned the whole party. One of the bunglers soon recovered presence of mind enough to unpocket a whisky-flask and deal a glass round; then, turning to the foxhunter, " Had it no been for your ill tongue ye suld hae had yin tae ; " which knowing dodge as effectually cooled the deathsman of the tods as if it had been a bucket of water.

How different soever their characters or dispositions may be, there is no doubt that men of the same occupation acquire a family likeness. Ratcatchers, "molemen," the old beadles of the Kirk, characteristically nicknamed "belltows," as well as cabmen, weavers, tailors, shepherds, &c., all are outwardly modelled into shape by the tools of the shop they work in. No better example of this general rule than the Highland

todhunter. His free step, bronzed half-savage
face, keen eye, and sinewy frame, tell tales of a
wild life among mountains and precipices, equally
callous to the winter blast or summer sun.

"Long, long ago," I was fishing with a companion of my boyish days in a quiet nook of "the
Pass of Glencroe," when we met a man such as I
have described, with a few ragged terriers at his
foot. He was the Arrochar foxhunter, and had
been searching the high-lying shielings for a stray
hound. My friend remarked that he had never
seen a finer specimen of the genus. With his
bold bearing, hardy weather-beaten face, erect
wiry frame, short round foot in hobnailed brogue,
lithe active gait, and long gun over his shoulder,
this Arrochar hillsman was the very embodiment
of Evan Dhu in 'Waverley.'

The foxhunter's occupation on Luss and Arrochar has been gone for many a long year, and I
never expected to see this last remnant of them
more. Two years since, when landing from the
Loch Lomond steamboat at Balloch, on the Leven,
a little, bent, very round-shouldered old man,
with whey-coloured weaver visage, a suit of

decent black clothes, splay feet cased in thin wellingtons, asked if I did not know Gregor Macgregor. His voice was weak, his step tottering and feeble—how could I know him, poor fellow? He was as unlike the Gregor of the mountains as a turkey buzzard to an eagle. He had completely succumbed, body and mind. There he was, stranded in the print - mill, like a vessel wrecked among the breakers—

> " Oh, how unlike her course at sea,
>   Or his free step on hill or lea ! "

I have noticed that foxes are less addicted to the higher cairns than badgers. The reason, no doubt, is, that the vixen likes to be in the midst of prey when rearing her litter. My sons and I, however, have sometimes flushed the dog-fox on the baldest mountain-tops. The sedate badger never wanders very far from its home, and indeed is unable, from its short thick legs and ungainly form, to travel any distance for prey. About the end of autumn their food of wasps or beehives, slugs, beetles, &c., is very plentiful, and is eked out by the carcasses of braxy sheep.

They then become extremely fat, and my boys
trapped two in October covered with lard like
pork. One of them being a very large male, with
bright silvery hair, I had him preserved for our
collection. After the second capture I put an
end to the raid on the harmless brocks.

The great abundance of blue hares, which form
the chief food of the foxes, frequently allures a
pair of golden eagles from the opposite hills of
Corrynge. They are the only ones of this district,
and always choose for their eyrie some one or
other of the cliffs between Glenfalloch and Bal-
quhidder. The quietness and extent of the hunting-ground have also emboldened the peregrine to
build yearly on the confines, while a male hen-
harrier constantly swept over the heather during
the last year of my lease.

Such are the wild fauna prowling over the
rugged frontier of the Glenfalloch shootings, the
background being filled up by the ptarmigan
hills. They are four in number—Ben Duchray,
Ben Oss, Ben Loy, and Ben Achly. The two
centre ones are the "surest find," and generally
have one or two packs of white grouse every good

breeding year. For these few birds there is such an amount of rocky and (unless to an experienced hillman) dangerous ground to be searched, that even with trained ptarmigan dogs, and working them hard to boot, many an enthusiastic sportsman may return without having stumbled on a single bird all day.

Certainly it is not mere love of shooting that can give excitement or piquancy to a wearisome West Highland ptarmigan range. Strip it of its scenery, labour, difficulty, and it is nothing; but a few brace of ptarmigan, with these adjuncts thrown into the scale, would outweigh, with every true lover of Highland shooting, the heaviest game-bag gathered with little trouble, sometimes even with little fatigue.

To sally forth alone on a distant and toilsome ptarmigan expedition had a peculiar charm for me. One could thus realise a modicum of the self-reliant independence,—nay, even some of the endurance of hardship,—at once the unfailing characteristic and the boast of the rovers among the American backwoods.

Even a successful day at white grouse on the

West Highland districts never produces an inconveniently heavy game-bag. An attendant, therefore, is little needed, except to give advice, which a man who knows the nature and habits of this bird, has a quick and keen eye, and a brace of steady dogs used to the sport, is far better without.

In the year 1862, grouse had bred badly (owing to late snows) on the Kuron, the wild stretch of moorland I have just sketched, and which forms the principal range of the Glenfalloch shootings. My second son and I had good sport, however, on the two smaller beats, averaging from 20 to 30 brace during August and the first weeks of September. The weather also had been very propitious till then, when it broke, and a fair day was a rarity. Wishing to spare the Kuron, and having shot down the full complement that the other moors would bear, I had for a fortnight been looking wistfully towards the ptarmigan hills. Each morning they were enclosed with fogs, and the weather itself was aptly described by an old Highland "kimmer" as "shoory, shoory, shoory, an' rain between."

On the 11th September, a rather too clear morning determined me to risk my "ptarmigan day." I had at that time two excellent rock-dogs, one a black setter with indomitable pluck to search every stony cairn, his assistant an old pointer of famed pedigree, and staid as Ben Loy itself.

With a game-pouch slung over my shoulder and the trusty canine coupled at heel, I left Glenfalloch door before eight o'clock. A short walk along the highroad leads to the rough steep path winding over the first height. Surrounded by natural strips of wood, and skirting the Kuron burn, whose dark and drumly linns raved from the rocky abyss, this track ended in the heathery morasses at the foot of the Kuron hill. Hitherto I had been threading the covert-haunts of roes and black-game, but now the route lay for eight long miles among the domains of grouse and deer.

Although the Kuron hill, from its very ruggedness, sometimes gave a short stretch of tolerably level walking, these eight miles of moorland were nevertheless one continued climb till they reached the base of Ben Loy. Sometimes a pack of grouse or a solitary old cock would rise within shot, but I prevented all unnecessary loading of the game-bag by carrying an empty gun.

The heather at last began to merge into green patches, and the granite boulders became more frequent. In place of starting up singly at inter-vals, the alpine hares showed in threes and fours on all the adjacent knolls, and in their midst was the fox's cairn, where the last spring litter had been destroyed.

Towering before me in solitary majesty, its crown of granite gleaming in the autumn sun, the sharp peaks and beetling scaurs of Ben Loy gave proof that the day's labour was only about to begin. The deceptive intervening heights and hollows made the mountain appear close before me, but there was still a good extent of ragged grass-ground between my stand-point and the first steep pull, which was really the base of the hill. This ground, blending into grass from heather, was a favourite resort of stray deer from the Black Mount Forest, so I took a resting sur-vey, meaning to profit by it the next opportunity. There were only, however, a few scattered sheep on the sky-line, and a shepherd with his collie stealing quietly down the glen.

Not until the first shoulder of Ben Loy is surmounted can the ptarmigan ground be said to begin. The green plant, as necessary to the existence of white grouse as heather to the red, then shoots up among the incessant rock and stone—some heaped into shapeless masses, forming gloomy caverns, but more often scattered regularly along the hill face, like the handiwork of some primeval giant.

I had just loaded, and was about to release my dogs, when from a crag above I detected two small heads peering down at my proceedings. Glad that my four-footed pair were still coupled, and feeling confident that no birds but those I was in pursuit of would be found so high, I only waited to satisfy myself by the motion of one of them that the two dark knobs were birds' heads, when, taking sure marks, I stalked round the rocks and came in on the opposite side. To my dismay, a brace of golden plover, in happy security, were within twenty yards of my gun muzzle! In place of stringing both sitting at one shot, with a contemptuous jerk I set free the dogs, when the plover flew screaming down the hill.

A few moments proved the prudence of this forbearance, whatever the motive; for Bob the setter had scarcely taken one sweep of the mountain scaur, when he dropped into a dead set. The pointer was also statue-like in a moment; but ere I moved a step, a pack of seven ptarmigan rose out of reach, and skirted the bald hill-face straight forward. I was marking their course when the eighth sprang up, but, taking the opposite direction, crossed me a long side-chance. I fired; but, if struck, the rapid and determined flight round the steep angle of the cliffs gave no encouragement to pursue.

The line of the pack, however, was more easily traced and followed; for although the mountain was as thickly studded with stones as a well-macadamised highway, there were no precipices and even few hill-scaurs to contend with. Hunting my dogs in little circles—now on one side, then on the other—I yet trusted my own eyes quite as much as their noses, and took good care never to lose my bearings of the exact line of my game.

Calculating the ordinary flight of the white grouse, I had now reached the limit where it was probable the pack might plump down, when, raising my head from the scrutiny of a tempting cairn, I saw the farther peaks enveloped in dense mist, and at the rate it was driving onwards the whole range would also in no time be engulfed, making the solitary being on the blank mountain nearly as helpless as the sons of Egypt amid the thick darkness that "could be felt."

Facing about, I sped before the grim pursuer with the desperate haste of an Indian from a jungle fire, and had just reached the trusty guidance of a well-known watercourse, when suddenly a slight breeze on my face gave token that the wind had changed. Instead of rushing through the hill-trough, the fog, arrested in mid course, was rolled into blacker masses and slowly retreating, while blinks of sunlight regained possession of the murky crags.

Very soon the whole line of hills looked low and blue as before, and the mist disappeared as mysteriously as it arose. The lost ground was quickly retraced, but I had scarcely reached the point where I was headed by the fog, when, casting my eyes over the heights above, there was the pack, some perched on the granite boulders and the rest on the ground, only a few gunshots off. The dogs were instantly "heeled in," and, slipping softly up, I was almost within reach when my game looked scared and flew. Only six, however, rose, and the seventh was no doubt in hiding among the stones. When laid on the scent, the dogs instantly stood firm, and at the same moment the ptarmigan flew, and was as quickly brought low.

The pack of six made straight for the first ground, and their pertinacious visitor followed, in the hope that if he obtained a third meeting they ought to be less shy of his advances. The rocks between me and the hollow where they were at feed when first discovered were rather hurried over than hunted, but all my vigilance and the utmost pains of my careful dogs found no trace of them there. My plan, therefore, was to take a wide circling cast both up and down the hill, and, gradually contracting it, leave " no stone unsearched " where they could possibly have hidden.

P

I had barely reached the outermost, and what appeared to me the least attractive, disc of my circle, when the setter pitched sharply down with that self-satisfied look back to his master which says as plainly as words, " I have them now." On getting to the dogs' side he rose and stepped briskly forward to the top of a mound, under which the six birds rose together. Two flew back again across the mountain, but four dashed downwards, making for the peak below. The whole lot were nearly out of reach, but I fired quick at the old cock of the four, when he dropped his legs and soon after towered and fell.

The three remaining birds being driven into lower and easier ground, there was every prospect, by following quickly, of soon coming on their traces again. After a flight, white grouse as well as red are much inclined to pitch down under what shepherds call "the snibs" (prominent points) of a hill. As soon, then, as I had descended to their line and given the dogs a fair wind, I began the quest of these excrescences, and very soon was cheered by both dogs drawing to a dead point. This time the game sprang fair, and

I dropped one dead with my first barrel and hit
another badly with the second.

The struck bird again dipped straight down-hill
and settled on the lowest shoulder of the mountain, where I had the good hap to mark it, while
the remaining one, flying high in a contrary direction, was of course given up. Having made out
the exact group of rocks where the disabled bird
sought shelter, I coupled the dogs and set off
down the steep. On the very brink of a crag,
and beautifully placed for a sitting chance, I soon
perceived a round grey ball. It was, however, so
precisely similar to many of the small stones
dotted around, that until the breeze ruffled a
feather I could not make certain of my game. At
once aware that if the bird was able to rise it
would dodge over the rocks without giving time
even for a snap, I made all safe by a still poking
shot.

By the downward course of the last bagged
birds, I again found myself below the rocky
steeps of the mountain face, but, being still
pretty fresh, was tempted to try for new game
on Ben Oss, instead of re-scaling Ben Loy after

the remains of the scattered pack. The day was wearing on; having, however, two brace in the bag, I sat down by a spring, and shared my crust with the dogs in calm content.

Ben Oss, which, although fully as steep and rugged, is not nearly so high as Ben Loy, always harbours a pack or two of white grouse, where, from the nature and lie of the rocks, they are both more easily found and followed.

In order to spare my dogs unnecessary fatigue, I kept them on the couple until well into the ptarmigan feeding-ground; but just when I had gained the southern ridge of the mountain, and was about to commence the range, two beings came suddenly into view, so ludicrously out of keeping with the savage scene that the very dogs stared at them with wonder. There they were in bright scarlet, working amidst the desolation with their instruments at the Government survey. When, in reply to my query whether they had seen ptarmigan, the Garibaldi apparition, with a decided Berkshire accent, described a large pack of grouse which they had "flushed among the 'eath," I turned sharply round, and was off in a moment.

Both sides of Ben Oss descend abruptly into rocky precipices. They can only be ranged to advantage, therefore, by keeping the crest of the hill, and inclining to either slope as the skill of the shooter suggests. Of course the game is easier found by the dogs on the windward side; but as all birds like shelter, a good and quick shot will get more, though not such fair chances, by hunting chiefly to leeward. On the present occasion a fair light breeze wafted along the mountain-top, equally favouring both ridges.

Carefully ranging the top, but always with a serpentine course first to one ridge then across to the other, I had nearly finished the search of the mountain from south to north ere I was rewarded by the statuesque profile of the pointer on the very summit of a crag, and at its base was the setter squatted firm, evidently close to his game. The birds rose from some rocks below the ridge, so when they darted over the precipice the chance was quick and difficult. One fell to the first shot, but the second was nearly out of reach. The pack only contained four, but as the remaining three skimmed round the northern bend of the hill into lower and smoother ground, I had little doubt of recovering them again.

On the flat where I had calculated, the pointer at once touched on the scent; but before he had time to settle, a brace of ptarmigan rose wild, and took a straight course for the adjoining mountain of Duchray. Confident of a shot at the third, I ran forward to where they had taken wing, but was again balked, for the setter came suddenly *down wind* on the other side, and poked up the bird at the very spot I had so hastily quitted! It laboured, however, being evidently touched by my second barrel in the preceding double shot, and, incapable of the daring flight of its companions, turned back on Ben Oss, and slunk into a " gully " close at hand. It was easily found —sprung at my feet, and dropped dead down the ravine.

The sun was now slanting behind the western hills, and, barring the short respite when " the hunter produced his scanty pittance at noon," I had walked hard since early morn. After so trying a day, three brace of ptarmigan on one's shoul-

der were not to be " made light of," so, turning
my back on their mountains, I plodded the homeward ten-mile walk through green morass and
over heathery brae, only reaching my own door
when the beetle began to drone and the bat to
fly.

THE COMMON DOTTEREL.

WHATEVER the reason, this bird is yearly becoming a rarer visitant to North Britain. Frequenting only a few favoured places, and ten days or a fortnight being the limit of its stay, no wonder that this beautifully-tinted variety is about as difficult to meet with as any of the whole plover tribe. Even in the palmy days of Pennant, samples of the dotterel killed in Britain were not very attainable, as the following anecdote, told me by an English clergyman, will serve to show.

When spending the winter at Great Malvern six years ago, this gentleman, being one of the directors of the Museum, was showing me the collection. I took occasion to ask him if there were any dotterels in the neighbourhood, as I had been trying for years to shoot one, but had never yet seen a single specimen in its wild state. "When I was a young man," said he, "Pennant made me the same complaint, and suggested that, in place of being called *common*, the bird deserved the title of the *uncommon* dotterel." Soon afterwards this clergyman procured and forwarded a specimen to Pennant. And now comes the remarkable part of the story. For thirty years he never met the great naturalist, who had been totally blind for some time. After this long interval, happening to be in the old man's company, he walked up to him and said, "I suppose I need hardly hope you will remember me, Mr Pennant?" The blind man thought for a moment, and then called out with sudden eagerness, "Ah! my friend of the dotterel!"

The usual time of the dotterel's arrival is from the 9th to the 14th of May, and they remain about ten days or a fortnight on their first ground before separating for the higher breeding-places. The nest is most difficult to find, and a dotterel's egg is therefore a great prize to the collector. They come to this country in "trips" of from five or six to a dozen, and pitch on undulating downs and hillocks near the sea. Rough grass and heather has less attraction for this bird than thin fallow fields. But the most favoured feeding-ground of all is a newly broken up and sown down field of old lea, where they seem to find the most abundant supply.

We were about to leave Edinburgh for our country home, when a note from the courteous and accomplished Baronet of Dunglass warned me that the dotterels had appeared. This was on the 12th of May of the present year. On the 14th I took the earliest train out, and was at Dunglass to breakfast. Directly after, the head-keeper and two assistants were in waiting; and by every means in his power my kind host had endeavoured to insure success.

We threaded the glorious woody ravine surrounding the baronial halls of Dunglass, and I then started on a most fascinating coast drive, with my old acquaintances the Bass and the May in the distance, while the far view to the south was bounded by the romantic outline of Fast Castle, whose battlements could be dimly traced.

At the side of the road was the ruin of a church, since used, or rather abused, as the grand emporium of a smuggling gang. Here many a Dirk Hatteraick of the Forth had found a safe and secret refuge for the contents of his lugger; and if the mouldering walls could speak, strange stories might they bring to light. Soon after we drove over Pease Bridge, the highest arch perhaps in Scotland. Looking down from it made one's head swim round.

The keeper had despatched one of his aide-de-camps to search the heights near the sea, but retained the other, as he, having noticed the arrival of the dotterels, could guide us to the fields where they had been feeding. We commenced our beat very systematically. Often in line, but sometimes separating, we quartered each field with the regularity of well-trained setters, and never left it while there was a corner untried. And in truth there was need for this carefulness, as our game, except when the variegated breast of an old male was turned towards us, was as like the colour of fallow or lea ground as a ptarmigan to the granite rock.

The birds had shifted, and the old sub began to look unhappy; not a trace of them where he had noted two small flocks on the 11th, and we had looked all the ground strictly. The day must certainly prove a failure unless the far scout was successful. We made for his heights, and saw him watching our approach. A wave of his arm prepared us for the good news that he had spied a flock of twelve, and hoped they were safe in the adjoining fallows. Again we were foiled by the restlessness of our quarry; for in place of alighting where the man supposed, the birds had flown southwards, as a dyke-mason informed us, and passed him within throw of his trowel.

The march we then continued to the extremity of our beat, but no appearance of the flock, when the keeper suggested, as a forlorn hope, that we should re-search the field where his assistant had seen the twelve so lately. An old man was putting up a gate in one of these fields. "Perhaps he may help us, like the mason," I suggested. "Oh! sir, he's frae the Hielants; he'll no ken them." "Donal, hae ye seen thae birds that flee a' thegither?" "There micht be plenty

wad pass me, but I couldna tell them frae
ithers."

A laugh with, or at, old Donald cheered us for
a look through the last two fields. Only three-
quarters of an hour now remained if I wished to
catch the afternoon return-train, and we had gone
over one field, and half the other, when the young
watcher halted and listened. I was instantly on
my guard, and heard for the first time in my life
the "twit, twit, twit" of the dotterel, and soon
the company of twelve careered overhead at a
great height. Contracting and lowering their
circles, they darted out of sight behind a knoll,
and we now felt sure they were snugly grounded
in the same field with ourselves.

The youngest assistant was on my left when
we began the search, which we had scarcely done,
when, only a gunshot beyond him, he discovered
the flock. A halt and sign brought me to his
side. Next me stood a brilliant male, and the
rest, a good deal scattered, were beyond him.
Getting the old cock in line with as many as
possible, I fired a raking charge out of my heavy
duck-gun. He lay dead, as well as a couple of

. hens on the further side of him. The rest wheeled round and round high in the air, and again lit in the same field. The keeper noted the spot, and brought me up to it. Again an old male was my aim; but getting the group better together, another cock and two hens also fell to this discharge.

Sir James's dog-cart was close at hand, so, selecting two brightly-plumaged cocks and two hens for my brother's collection and my own, I left Dunglass and returned to Edinburgh by the middle of the afternoon, much gratified with so agreeable a day, and the possession of so long-coveted a prize.

THE WILDS OF SUTHERLAND.

ALTNAHARRA—DURNESS—SCOURIE—INCHNADAMFF.

MY first sight of Sutherland was in the summer of 1823; but what changes have these forty-three years wrought on this remote and primitive land! So far as I remember, there were then no white-faced sheep, and the moors and mountains were grazed by the old-fashioned blackfaces, interspersed with groups of "black cattle," the picturesque hirsel of the glens.

The savage precipices had tenfold interest as the constant haunts of golden eagles or peregrine falcons, while most of the sea-cliffs or lonely mountain tarns were associated with eyries of the erne or the osprey.

The rank and luxuriant heather had not then

been consumed to accommodate the vast flocks of Cheviots; the grouse were regularly distributed and healthy; while old deer with noble heads were far more common than in these modern days of cost and preservation, when numbers are made to atone for lack of size and high bearing.

The so-called vermin have disappeared, and no wonder. Like Indian scalps, a bribe is paid down by the shooting tenants for the head of each winged or footed creature of prey; and as this blood-money graduates in value from the nobler to the meaner birds or animals, of course the skill and cupidity of the keepers is chiefly directed to those magnificent specimens long ago driven to remote Highland tracts, but now in a fair way of being extirpated altogether.

The "iron road" now ends at Bonar Bridge, on the confines of Sutherland; so, in order to penetrate the lonesome straths and mountain roads of this sheep and deer grazed province, my son and I hired a neat little waggonette from Ardgay.

After baiting at Lairg, the first day's drive brought us to Altnaharra at half-past seven in the evening. The inn was exactly in the same state of cleanliness, order, and comfort as on my last visit, nine years since; and my old acquaintance, Harry Munro, the landlord, as civil and obliging as ever.

A course of fine weather had dried up the streams, but as there was some dead water at the foot of the feeding-burn of Loch Naver, my son borrowed Harry's nondescript rod to try for any stray loch-trout that might be feeding in this estuary.

The chief object of our northern tour being to collect varieties for the museum, we had not, in the face of so long a drought, added the encumbrance of fishing-rods, but a fly-book always forms part of our travelling gear, let the weather be wet or dry. In defiance of the remonstrances of Harry's farm man, who insisted they were "ower sma'," the fisher selected three flies to suit his own fancy, and by half-past nine landed twenty loch-trout—amply sufficient for a supper that night, for a remove before the excellent roast beef of our next day (Sunday) dinner, and for an adjunct to Monday's breakfast before leaving for Durness. When our trap was packing, Harry

Q

quietly stepped up to me and asked, "What flees the young gentleman fished wi', as he had never seen so many troots ta'en oot o' that bit water before."

Hail-showers at night, the hill-tops white in the morning, and keen east wind, changed the temperature from summer to almost winter again. However, before reaching "bonnie Strathmore" the sun had struggled out, and shed its glory on that lonely glen. At the foot of it we fed the horse, and walked on before up the steep hill on the road to Durness, a stretch of at least five miles. The road skirted the old forest of Reay, but we were never out of the seemingly endless region of whitefaced sheep. At five in the evening the fishing village of Durness showed in the distance, and we had travelled between forty and fifty miles among the Sutherland mountains without sighting either a red deer or an eagle.

Our driver, besides being a very intelligent lad, had been employed in various capacities all over the county. With great precision he pointed out the marches, described the shooting-beats and their tenants, knew the different proprietors, as

well as the names of most of the hill-lochs or
mountain-streams. From constant yearly report
of the different shooting and fishing bags, he had
also formed a pretty shrewd guess of the sporting
capabilities of the land and water we skirted, as
well as of the sporting skill of those who rented
it. This forenoon he was more than usually
demonstrative at a fox's cairn close to the road.
A few years since he had been a hind on this
farm, and assisted at the night-watches for reynard among these rocks, which, he assured us,
were catacombed for a hundred yards along the
mountain face. A short distance before, he
pointed out a precipice where his master the
farmer ("who had ower muckle whusky") had
been pitched over with his gig. The horse and
gig were dashed to pieces, but the farmer was
miraculously thrown forward on a green mound,
and escaped with a slight bruise.

The bold rocks about half-way between Durness
and "the Cape" (Wrath) had attracted us to this
wild coast. They are the favoured resort of myriads of sea-birds, including the white-tailed eagle.
" If ye had been here last week it wad hae been

grand," said the weather-beaten coastman, "but we daurna ventur in this easterly swell."

The cold dull "haar" seemed fairly set in, as there was no change in the night, so we drove down a distance of twenty miles to Scourie, where the island of Handa, with its beetling cliffs, attracts the same description of sea-fowl as the rocks below Durness.

Although the swell on the outward and exposed rocks of Handa would prevent our skirting them unless the wind changed, still the old fisherman, Macleod, assured us that the sheltered creek and bays between Handa and the mainland often attracted curious sea-birds. The old man was familiar with the commoner sorts, had sometimes noticed stormy petrels there, and casually mentioned what he called "sea-pigeons." We at first thought he meant rock-doves; but the bird he meant had red feet, *a red bill,* and dived. Its colour also was black, with a white patch on the wing. The black guillemot, thought I; but then the red bill. "Are you sure of the colour of this bill?" He passed his word that it was bright as vermilion.

To secure this red-bill I eagerly ordered his boat to be ready at nine next morning. "What can that bird be?" I said so often during the evening, that my son compared my curiosity to that of the old Caithness laird, who never could rest without knowing everything about everybody. When travelling north with a friend, he stayed the night at a small inn. "Ye'll be frae Caithness?" says he to the maid-of-all-work. "No," rather curtly. "Frae Sutherland, then?" "No," a little sulkily. "Ou, I hae't; ye're frae Ross-shire?" "No," still. "Ye maun be frae the Mearns, then?" The "No" was nearly smothered by the slamming of the door. All the evening the laird was thoughtful and abstracted, and when he took his candle to go to bed, made the earnest appeal to his companion—"Whar can that lassie be frae?"

Macleod honestly told us that the sea-eagle had not built on Handa last season, nor this, so far as he knew. He gave their correct titles to the common guillemots, razor-bills, puffins, cormorants green and black, &c., and was only a little confused about the gulls. What, then, could this sea-pigeon be? If I could only get him to give way on the carnation beak—but catch him!

The breeze had lulled, but it was still from the east. The two boatmen, therefore, were still unable to say whether we could round the outer rocks of Handa until they cleared the farthest mainland cape. They then began to shake their heads,—" There was ower great a swell to gang within shot o' the cliffs, but we might try the landlocked creek and bays first, an' maybe it wad moderate by the evenin'." The calm water, too, was best for " sea-pigeons " and stormy petrels.

With slow pull the men crept·along the coast, while, on rounding each peak into a fresh bay, Macleod protested he had never " gaen ower sae muckle water" without spying the mysterious red-bill. At length my son asked for the telescope, and on returning it carelessly remarked, " There are a couple of black guillemots." Macleod was alive in a moment—" That's the sea-pigeon." To satisfy him we rowed towards the birds. One rose out of reach, and the other (a very distant shot) was dropped by the No. 4, its bill, to our boatman's chagrin, black as ebony! Unlike many of his superiors in birth and culture, this poor Highlander's radiant freak of fancy was, I am convinced, neither premeditated nor wilful.

As the surf, in place of abating, was coming in stronger, we gave up all hope of circling the island. A landing on it was easily made, and we proceeded to the erne's rock. The alarm shot only brought out some rock-birds, but the eagle, as Macleod suspected, had forsaken her eyrie. A pair of peregrines used to nestle in the next cliff, but they also had deserted their stronghold.

Man's persecution of these birds of prey must have been constant and keen ere they could be induced to desert spring quarters so abundantly supplied with food for their nestlings. Within shot were tier on tier and rank on rank of razor-bills, guillemots, coulter-nebs, ranged like the defenders of a beleaguered fortress. The crest of one stack of detached rock rising abruptly from old ocean had never been trodden by human foot. Sunning themselves on this turf, a colony of lesser black-backed gulls lay, or rolled about, in heedless, conscious security. On the sides were thousands of cliff-birds so shockingly tame that I desired Macleod to pitch a few stones to try to enliven the dormant mass. At the second throw he killed one, which dropped into the yawning abyss, while only a few of its nearest neighbours deigned to leave their perch.

On looking into the awful chasm, we distinctly perceived the large green single egg on several of the ledges, but only one *pair* of eggs, and these were half the size of the others, and whitish-coloured.

As we already possessed all the specimens we noticed on and around Handa, the sail was soon hoisted for Scourie, and in the afternoon and evening a rugged drive through the mountains to Inchnadamff completed a thoroughly enjoyable day.

Near the top of an Assynt mountain we encountered a delightfully patriarchal " flitting." As the steep road was also narrow, our driver had to pull up in order to let the caravan pass, so we had full time to admire its simple order and discipline. First came two sons, each guiding a pony and light cart loaded with beds and furniture; then one of the daughters leading the

milch cow. Next came her sister, skilfully driving four sheep with the aid of their two collies.
The hale mother now trudged forward with a
hen in her apron. Lastly followed the patriarch,
like Jacob, with staff in hand, and at a sufficient
distance behind the procession to give him a good
view of the whole. There could not be a more
contented or healthy-looking family, and the
stately father, with his ruddy face browned by
the mountain blasts, was a noble type of the
Highland shepherd.

A half-way ferry and constant succession of
steep hills between Scourie and Inchnadamff,
lengthened the way so much that the long day
had faded into twilight ere we were housed for
the night. My former fishing-guide of Loch
Assynt, who was then the Duke's game-preserver,
is now landlord at Inchnadamff. If any one
could give a hint about a bird we have long
wished for, John Sutherland, our host, is the man.

We already possessed specimens of the great
northern diver, both in spring and winter plumage, also of the red-throat; but black-throated
divers, although pretty common in the northern

lochs, are far more rare in the waters of the central or western Highlands. When consulting John about this bird, an open vehicle most opportunely drove up. This was the Duke's superintendent of the Scourie division of Sutherland, who had come down to Assynt to settle the marches between the Sutherland and Tarbat estates.

Mr M., with hearty Highland warmth, promoted the object of our tour. He suggested that Sutherland himself should accompany us to a small loch where a pair of black-throats yearly hatched, and we were, if possible, to shoot the male, when the female, having only begun to lay, would soon provide another mate.

Next morning we drove to this lochan, with its prettily-wooded islets, on two of which Sutherland proposed my son and I should lie in hiding whilst he moved our quarry.

Snugly ensconced among the bushes of the two mid islets, we soon perceived the pair emerge from the reeds of the furthest bay, and John's boat guiding them if possible to our cross-fire. The creatures, of course, kept close together when taken in rear, and, coasting the mainland, seemed inclined to shirk a passage between the islets. This move forced me to change ground to the opposite side of my island. I soon, however, saw them cross over and make for the very passage we had set them. Instantly regaining my first ambush, I had a full view of the splendid birds. In their gorgeous spring plumage their feathers absolutely gleamed in the sunlight. Rounding the point of my islet, they turned into the straits between the guns. My son had seen me creep away to the other side of my ambuscade, but was too much occupied with the divers to notice my return. He therefore thought that all depended on his gun, however distant the chance.

The birds were almost within reach when both dived, but soon came to the surface again, a near shot from me, and consequently a far one from him. A perceptible difference in size enabled both of us to mark the male, and my duck-gun had covered him, while my finger was just touching the trigger, when an opposite shot prostrated him on the surface. My feeling at the moment was like a person going down-stairs in the dark, and reaching the last step before he expected. The object is gained sooner than intended, or even wished !

Unmixed pleasure at the brilliant prize floating on the waters quickly followed; and when Sutherland rowed to land with the finest male specimen I had. ever seen of this most beautiful of all divers, my content was complete.

Our landlord supplied us with a couple of small rods, but none of the flies in our book were " cut out " for this loch.   In about two hours and a half, however, we brought into the boat thirty fine red trout, which were delicious at table. With orthodox flies a hundred fish to each rod is an average good day's work ; how sumptuously, therefore, the black-throats must have fared every day !

Next morning Mr M. gave a most graphic account of *his* sport on the marches.   Of course he had a number of the aged natives as witnesses, and some of these ancient Celts grew quite fierce in their Gaelic disputes with each other.   One venerable Sutherland oracle frantically tottered up to the arbitrator with " I wonder, sir, to see you allow Ross to beat Sutherland after this fashion!"

A most interesting and valuable map of the county was shown us by Mr M. It was discovered in Dunrobin Castle by the late Duke, and is entirely finished by the pen. Ships stand for the sea — cattle, &c., represent land; and in addition to its topographical merits as a map, the whole is executed with exquisite artistic skill.

The drive from Inchnadamff to our first starting-point, the inn of Ardgay, was chiefly through Sir C. Ross's estates. This day, on a lonely stretch of moorland, a sea-eagle crossed our path. It kept long in view, and its wild and wayward wheels gave life and interest to a barren, dreary tract. This was the first royal bird we discovered during our tour; and although the course lay quite round the forest of Loch Stack, the deer seem to have avoided the sheep-runs, and kept strictly to their reserved ground. On my last visit to this county nine years since, although never beyond the bounds of sheep pasturage, we noticed deer almost every day.

Reaching Ardgay about five P.M., we told the landlord our intention of hiring on to Tain, in order to try the sea estuaries, where we had noticed some sheldrakes from the railway carriages the previous week. These creeks being close to Tain, and the tide suiting, we were anxious, if possible, to secure a male of this ornamented duck, still required to complete a case.

On explaining the plan to mine host, he ordered out a fresh horse, quietly remarking, " Now, sir, I am not going to charge you anything for this hire." An honourable and spirited fellow like this deserves to prosper in his calling.

The tide was three-quarters ebb when we pulled up at the first bay, where, feeding among the plashy sands and sea-ware, a sheldrake and his mate were distinctly made out with the telescope. As these birds are sometimes curiously stupid and tame, my son was not without hope of stalking them, even in such disadvantageous ground. To our surprise they saved him the trouble, by taking wing in a straight line for the gun. On nearing, they shied off a little, and crossed at the distance of about seventy yards.

He fired, and the drake dropped nearly to the gravel, then, recovering himself, separated from his mate (which flew seaward), and laboured over a corn-field, repassing the shooter a second time at long distance—was again hit, after which he struggled round a landward height.

We quickly followed with the retriever, but never came on his traces afterwards. No doubt where he pitched, there he lay and died. We saw no more of these ducks, and were chagrined to lose so fine a bird, as the nut above his bill was quite perceptible when he flew past, and proved him to be in brightest spring feather.

Next morning we left Tain by the railway, coming down for the first time the charming route by Braemar, Kingussie, Rannoch, Blair-Atholl, and Perth, reaching Glasgow in the gloaming.

THE END.